THE RUSH HOUR COOK™

presents

Weekly WONDERS

She's everything *that Martha isn't!*

by BROOK NOEL

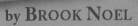

WEEKLY MENUS COMPLETE WITH GROCERY LISTS FOR TODAY'S BUSY FAMILY

Other books in the Rush Hour Cook™ Series

The Rush Hour Cook: Presto Pasta $5.95
The Rush Hour Cook: Effortless Entertaining $5.95
The Rush Hour Cook: Family Favorites $5.95
The Rush Hour Cook: One-Pot Wonders $5.95

COMING IN SEPTEMBER 2003
The Rush Hour Cook: Very-Tasty Vegetarian $5.95
The Rush Hour Cook: Healthy at Home $5.95

OTHER BOOKS BY BROOK NOEL
I Wasn't Ready to Say Goodbye: surviving coping and healing
    after the sudden death of a loved one (co-authored with
    Pamela D. Blair) and Companion Workbook
Back to Basics: 101 Ideas for Strengthening Our Children and
    Our Families
The Single Parent Resource
Shadows of a Vagabond

To order visit your favorite bookseller or order online at
www.championpress.com

ISBN 1-891400-14-2
LCCN: 2002111681

Cover photo credit: Craig Heun
Rush Hour Cook Logo Design: Quintero Designs
Interior Illustrations: Johnny Caldwell
Cover Design: Saul Fineman

10 9 8 7 6 5 4 3 2 1
This book was printed in the United States of America.

For multiple sales or group discounts contact Champion Press, Ltd, 4308 Blueberry Road,
Fredonia, WI 53021 – www.championpress.com

DEDICATION

There are so many people to thank on this little page that is read by so few! I hope everyone reading this book will send a thank you and good thought for each of the people who were so vital in this process...

Samantha Noel...my precious seven-year-old daughter, who remains my biggest fan. This book wouldn't be possible without you. Thanks for your help in researching, writing, tasting and copy-editing! You are life's greatest treasure. "I love you mountains."

Andy Stowers...my wonderful husband and life partner, who never gives up on me—even when I'm ready to give up on myself! Thank you for being my anchor.

My Mom...who has helped to prune and tweak my writing and my personality since childhood.

My dear friends, Sara Pattow, Carrie Myers Smith, Rhonda Levitch and MaryAnn Koopmann.... Thanks for supporting me in all that I do. You are all wonderful inspirations to me and I appreciate you more than I can possibly convey in a lifetime.

To my "Champion Staff" who manage to meet challenge after challenge with a champion attitude and cheerful spirit. I couldn't do it without you!

Also to David Quintero for his innovative design abilities and help with the Rush Hour Cook logo and Johnny Caldwell for his comical Rush Hour illustrations (and great sense of humor!)

Lastly, to my two goldfish, Tom & Jerry... (just kidding, just wanted to see if anyone was still reading!)

Actually, my first and last thanks are to God, who has shown me that all things are possible.

EENIE-MEENIE-MINEY-MOE...
TWO WAYS TO USE THIS BOOK

In a nutshell, I created this book out of tremendous need. I *needed* to find some sanity in my crazy life. My daughter and husband needed sanity, too. The easiest place to connect and unwind seemed to be over dinner. With that discovery, we made a goal of implementing the family dinner hour in our home. It didn't work. What I soon learned was that without a comprehensive map we would never get to our destination. Sometimes we didn't have the food we needed on hand, other times we didn't have enough food that everyone liked, and still other times, the meal preparation was so tedious we wouldn't be able to sit down until 9 PM! If something was going to change, it was up to me to change it. I began accumulating all the recipes we liked in one place. I started adding new recipes. Little by little, *Weekly Wonders* was coming to fruition. Now this book serves as our lifeline to a simple and sane dinner hour during which we can connect and enjoy one another. I believe *Weekly Wonders* can do the same for you and your family.

WEEKLY WONDERS ROUTE #1: You can, as I do, just grab a weekly menu, based on what's on sale at your local market or what you happen to have on hand. Check off any items you already have from the grocery list (you'll find the grocery list at the end of each weekly plan). Grab the other ingredients and you're good to go.

WEEKLY WONDERS ROUTE #2: Or, if you like to plan your own menus and are simply looking for quick easy meals, no problem. Consult the Make Your Own Menu Index on page 227. You'll find other hints and tips for creating your own *Weekly Wonders* menus on page 209.

Okay, enough preamble, let's get to revolutionizing your kitchen and changing the way you cook! Here's to many shared family dinners at both your home and mine!

TABLE OF CONTENTS

5 / Eenie-Meenie-Minie-Moe: How to Use this Book
7 / Table of Contents
8 / Recipe Menu Index

Part One
Tips, Ideas and Wisdom
from a Rush Hour Kitchen

13 / Chapter One: The Birth of the Rush Hour Cook
21 / Chapter Two: The Rush Hour Guide to Healthy Eating
27 / Chapter Three: A Balanced Breakfast
29 / Chapter Four: 10 Dazzling Dressings and Marvelous Marinades
34 / Chapter Five: Stocking up On Snacks
37 / Chapter Six: The Art of Bulk Cooking
40 / Chapter Seven: Practically Instant Family Dinners (just add family)
44 / Chapter Eight: Steaming Success
46 / Chapter Nine: Dazzling Desserts
54 / Chapter Ten: Soothing Smoothies

Part Two
The Weekly Plans

59 / Week One
67 / Week Two
73 / Week Three
81 / Week Four
89 / Week Five
101 / Week Six
111 / Week Seven
121 / Week Eight
129 / Week Nine
139 / Week Ten
145 / Week Eleven
151 / Week Twelve
159 / Week Thirteen

165 / Week Fourteen
173 / Week Fifteen
183 / Week Sixteen
191 / Week Seventeen
197 / Week Eighteen
205 / Week Nineteen

The Weekly Meal Plans
Use this section for easy reference of the meal plans
available to you. Find one you like,
turn to the recipes and enjoy!

WEEK ONE	WEEK TWO
Quick and Crispy Chicken Mash-It Potatoes • Ham and Swiss Pizza Fruit Salad • Easy Pasta Toss Choose-A-Way Breadsticks • "Pita Soup" and Calzone Sandwich • Feisty Fiesta Casserole Simple Salad French Bread	Covered Chicken Simple Salad • Chicken and Potatoes Skillet Rosemary Broccoli • Almost Oriental Noodle Dish • Chicken Stroganoff Simple Salad • French Bread Pizzas
WEEK THREE	WEEK FOUR
Taco Nacho Salad • Kid-Friendly Sloppy Joes Pretty Pasta Salad • Make-Mine-A-Melt Potato Wedges • Scrumptious Swiss Strata • Chicken in Whine Sauce Poupon Potatoes	Chicken Tenders Potato Wedges • Parmesan Rotini Quesadilla Bites • Presto Primavera Corn on the Cob • Perfect Pork Chops Dijon Potatoes • 2+2+2+2 = Turkey Store-Bought Stuffing Glorious Green Beans

WEEK FIVE	WEEK SIX
Classic Chicken Bake Sugar Carrots • Presto Mac Very Garlic-y Chicken Caesar Salad • Christmas Eve Chili • Sammy's Favorite Noodle Bake • Let-Me-Soak Chicken Cheesy Scalloped Spuds	Presto Pasta Aunt Joan's Fruit Cup • Delightfully Dijon Chicken Sour Cream Pasta • Super Stroganoff Supper Simple Salad • Turkey and Stuffing Casserole • Stand-by Spaghetti Choose-A-Way Breadsticks
WEEK SEVEN	WEEK EIGHT
Pot Roast Perfection Cinnamon Sweet Potatoes • Shepherd's Pie Sweet and Sour Carrots • Magnificent Mac Pretty Peach Cup • Cool Crispy Chicken Baked Potato Bonanza • Steak Soup Simple Salad	Honey Chops Twice as Nice Veggie Rice • Bowtie Bonanza Tomato Bread • Speedy Salisbury Steak Ranch Potatoes • Chicken and Vegetable Bake I-Slaved-All-Day Biscuits • Chicken Fettuccini Dijon Awesome Applesauce

WEEK NINE	WEEK TEN
Tasty Turkey Slices Breaded Mozzarella Sticks • Turkey Pot Pie Berry Compote • Lasagna Rolls Bedazzling Breadsticks • Rockin' Rotini Rosemary Broccoli • Chicken Parmesan Aunt Sally's Potatoes	Ham and Potatoes Glorious Green Beans • Stacked Chops Baked Potato Bonanza • Hammy Noodles Glorious Green Beans • No Red-Sauce Spaghetti Bedazzling Breadsticks Simple Salad • Grilled Honey Chicken Easy Pasta Toss
WEEK ELEVEN	WEEK TWELVE
Perfect Parmesan Chicken Perfect Parmesan Potatoes • Italian Chicken in a Flash Robust Rice Pilaf • Kids-Love-It Casserole Simple Salad • Taco Pizza • Cheese Pizza Please	Hip and Healthy Stroganoff Rosemary Broccoli • Cheddar-y Turkey Casserole • Marvelous Meatloaf Potato Pancakes • Mushroom and Beef Pasta Tomato Bread • Soy-Sketti Marvelous Mushroom Rice

WEEK THIRTEEN	WEEK FOURTEEN
Ham and Pasta Bake	Really Good, Creative Tacos
•	•
Chicken Cordon Blue	Chili Tortilla Pie
Twice Baked Potatoes	•
•	Chicken Broth
Cajun Chicken	Angel-Hair Pasta
Basic Fettuccini Pasta	Ricotta Pesto Bread
•	•
Grilled Cheese Please	Lemon Broiled Chicken
Funky Fries	Lyonnaise Potatoes
•	•
Gnarly Barley Casserole	Cheese Stuffed Manicotti
	Tomato Bread
	Simple Salad

WEEK FIFTEEN	WEEK SIXTEEN
Beef Enchilada Casserole	Speedy Chicken Fajitas
•	Twice as Nice Veggie Rice
Cajun Flank Steak	•
Twice-as-Nice Veggie Rice	Marinated Flank Steak
•	Baked Potato Bonanza
Shredded Beef Sandwiches	•
Awesome Apple Cobbler	Chicken-Ricotta Pasta Bake
•	Corn on the Cob
Noodle Bake	•
Parmesan Garlic Toasts	Chicken and Cheese Enchiladas
•	Fiesta Corn
Tucson Style Pork Roast	•
Cinnamon Baked Apples	Ground Beef Pita Pizza
	Choice of Steamed Veggies

WEEK SEVENTEEN	WEEK EIGHTEEN
Taco Revival Corn Casserole •	Broccoli Bake Easy Pasta Toss •
Linguini With Herb Butter Tomato Bread •	Roast Beef and Gravy Potato Squares •
Lemon Angel-Hair Pasta Parmesan-Garlic Toasts •	Pizza Burgers Potato Wedges •
Hamburger Clubs Funky Fries •	Toss-it-Together Lasagna Choose-A-Way Breadsticks •
Basil Chicken with Wild Rice Rosemary Broccoli	Spaghetti Pie Simple Salad

WEEK NINETEEN

Nice Chicken and Rice
Sugar Carrots

•

Chicken and Mushrooms
Garlic Ties

•

Lazy Cordon Bleu
Robust Rice Pilaf

•

Ham and Swiss
Crescent Pouches
Potato Wedges

•

Baked Orange-Ginger Chicken
Potato Pile

1.

TIPS, WISDOM AND IDEAS

FROM A RUSH HOUR KITCHEN

*from the original Rush Hour Cook
mini-volume, Family Favorites....*

CHAPTER ONE

THE BIRTH OF THE RUSH HOUR COOK

This all started very innocently. I am the owner of a successful, small publishing company, and while talking to a trusted friend and colleague, I realized there was a need for quick dinner solutions with simplistic ingredients and surreal taste. After talking to many home cooks, I realized there was a need for "little books"—not tomes with 401 recipes for sugar cookies and 837 variations of chili. No, what people needed, I discovered, were simple recipes for good food, in an assessable, user-friendly book. Busy moms and dads could toss it in their purse or briefcase, decide what to eat while driving home (or arranging Johnny's soccer schedule), or take it to the grocery store since it would include complete grocery lists. It didn't take me long to decide that Champion Press™ would publish just such a book.

What wasn't so clear was who would author this new, indispensable guide. Champion has a slew of successful cookbook authors. While trying to decide which writer to assign to the project, a friend of mine suggested that I author the series. Keep in mind that this same friend, when in college, witnessed my attempt to microwave a non-microwaveable pizza, and said nothing when I forgot to remove the plastic wrap. Needles to say, my lack of domesticity has long been evident. (I can't iron anything without creating more wrinkles than I started with; although I think this has to do more with my being left-handed than my actual skill level.) I do not sort laundry by colors, fabrics or labels. And, more than once, I have been spotted purchasing finger JELL-O® pre-made at the deli. So I asked her, "Why on earth should I write a cookbook series?"

"Well," she said simply. "Think about it... you are the absolute Queen of Incapable Cooking." (I tried not to glare at her as I listened to this rationale.) She continued, "In order for you to find 30-50 recipes—you will have to cook 200-300—*at least!* You will have to taste-test more than probably any other cook on the planet! Plus, if _you_ can cook something quickly—and have it taste good...well...then...it's fool proof!" she rambled excitedly.

"Huh," I replied.

While I wasn't thrilled with this exchange, I had to admit that her reasoning had merit. Earlier in the week, I had watched my daughter excitedly announce to fellow grocery shoppers that it "must be a holiday!" When another shopper stated that she wasn't aware of any holidays, Sammy quickly explained, "My mom is cooking from a real-live recipe... not a box! It must be a holiday! She has never done that before." I smiled meekly, holding up my canister of marjoram in defense. The other woman snickered and cast a condescending stare.

Later that night, I brought the subject up to my husband and mother while I was busy wrapping leftovers in the kitchen. "Mom—did you buy this plastic wrap at the dollar store?" I asked while fighting with the plastic and its supposedly quick-cut-tooth-grabber on the box edge.

"Yes—why?" she asked from the table.

"It doesn't really work so well," I grumbled while yanking yet another yard in an attempt to secure my dish. It took about 18 yards and two sailor knots to secure the plastic to the bowl. My husband was entering the kitchen just as I secured the last knot.

"Need some help, honey?"

"I'm fine; it's just the wrap." Of course, he then proceeded to wrap three more dishes with metric precision that didn't waste a millimeter of the dreaded plastic.

"Anyway," I said, returning to the table. "What would you guys think of me writing a cookbook?" My husband made this familiar noise that he makes when he thinks someone is telling a joke, but isn't sure. My mother tried to look engrossed by the television—even though it wasn't turned on. "Well?" I urged.

"Is something wrong with the television?" my mother asked.

"It's not turned on," I said simply.

"I better look into that," Andy said as he rose. Without so much as a backward glance, they both left the table.

In that moment, *The Rush Hour Cook*™ was born.

It hasn't been an easy road, but I'll admit I had ulterior motives for writing this series. I am energetic and frequently work out through the martial arts and running. While my physical endurance is strong, my diet appalls most people (and it actually appalls me as well.) I can live for a week on nothing more than soft pretzels and Twizzlers™. This is not something that makes me proud. My life is a zoo of insanity that allows very little time for cooking let alone making frequent trips to the grocery store. But as an Editor and Publisher, I frequently read about health issues, preservative dangers and other influences our diet has on our body. I wanted to see if I would actually feel better if I found my vitamins in food, instead of the buy-one-get-one-free sale at GNC™. I also wanted to minimize my risk of future health ailments. After all, cook or no cook, I am a mom—and I want to be around

many, many years to enjoy my beautiful child and family. I hope that throughout this process I can pass on some healthful knowledge and good habits along the way.

My last motive for authoring this series is to recreate the family dinner in my home. It's not uncommon for me to work 12 to 14 hour days. The thought of cooking at the end of an exhausting workday is about as intriguing as joining the Polar Bear Club and jumping into frigid-degree water. Yet, without that meal to bond us as a family each night, we all too often go our separate ways. My daughter will grab a snack here or there, I will eat while reading something from my briefcase and my husband will grab a bite on his way home from the office or just eat an extra-large lunch. Our few precious hours at home together, become invaded by diversions. But I noticed when I did cook (those two or three times a year) or when my mother would come over and cook, we would all sit around the table and talk and enjoy and share.

I truly think that one of the biggest problems facing the American family today is the loss of the family-dinner hour. Think about it—decades ago we shared two, if not three, meals together daily. These were basically mini-family-meetings, nourishing both body and soul. Now, statistics show we are fortunate to sit down together twice a week—to share a meal, much less linger over it!

In the end, I accepted my friend's challenge to write a cookbook series. I tried a lot of recipes, variations and methods. More food saw the garbage disposal than the pages of this book. But you will find within these pages the best-of-the-best recipes. Each recipe has been carefully tested for taste and time-saving ability. In addition, I created the Five Rules of Rush Hour Recipes and posted them on my cupboard. Any recipe that made it into this book had to meet the strict guidelines found on the following page:

THE FIVE RULES OF RUSH HOUR RECIPES:

1. All ingredients are may be pronounced accurately through the phonetic use of the English Language.

2. Each ingredient can be located in the market without engaging in a full scale scavenger hunt.

3. No list of ingredients shall be longer than the instructions.

4. Each recipe has to be durable enough to survive me, the Queen-of-Incapable–Cooking, and elicit a compliment at meal's end.

5. My finicky child will eat it—or some portion of it. I've learned not to be too picky on this one. Often I separate out part of the meal during preparation and customize it to her taste.

I dedicated myself to making this series one that you will cherish, love and refer to again and again. It has accomplished my aforementioned goals for a return to the family-dinner hour and easy, healthy eating.

And so began my journey into the world of food preparation. Much to all my friends' and family's amazement, I'm still cooking! In this volume I've taken my obsessive need for order and combined it with my quest for quick-cooking fare. Every section of this book is a menu for a week, complete with a shopping list. Since my recipes tend to be pretty palatable (they have to be to survive as many taste-testers as we went through) it will be easy for you to just grab a week that looks appealing, copy the shopping list, and you're off. No planning. No staring at an empty cabinet in horror. No wondering what on earth you can make with only year-old Bisquick® and a can of tomato paste. You won't need magic or luck to create a family dinner if you subscribe to the *Weekly Wonder Plans* within this book.

You'll notice that I only put five dinners in a week. The way I figure it, even the most organized of families are going to have one night where everyone is heading different directions, and one night that you opt to grab a bite on the run. For this reason, I went with five recipes per week so you wouldn't end up with spoiled groceries, and I, in turn, with a bunch of "not-so-fannish" fan mail.

THE RUSH HOUR COOK CLUB

If you haven't joined already make sure to stop by www.rushhourcook.com and join our free cooking club. You'll enjoy prizes, contests and more recipes!

If you are one of the lucky ones who enjoys seven meals at home, simply make a bit extra or use the other nights to make something your family has suggested. Or, better yet, let *your family* make something *you* have chosen.

CHAPTER TWO

THE RUSH HOUR GUIDE TO HEALTHY EATING

As you move through this book you'll see that the menus feature both meat and meatless dishes. I subscribe to the belief that we can survive without shoveling loads of red meat and starches into our system. That's not to say I'm a carbo addict—but I am not a protein pusher either. I have had a long and turbulent relationship with food. I'll spare you the gory details but trust me when I say finding a healthy eating plan that is also fulfilling has not been easy.

I have tried diets where I have consumed protein by the pound and likewise I've tried diets where I consumed pounds of pasta. I've read studies where both plans offered many benefits—and likewise I've read studies which state both plans will surely erode the body. I've read that I should drink gallons of water, only to grab another magazine that tells me it will mess up my electrolytes. I've tried diets where I ate by food group,

WOMEN IN WELLNESS™

One great stride in creating my healthy lifestyle came with the help of Carrie Myers Smith and her Women in Wellness™ service. After her own turbulent relationship with food, Carrie discovered and implemented a successful coaching system. Carrie helps women to set and achieve realistic goals. Then she helps build on each goal until you experience a complete makeover in any area of your life. Her wellness approach focuses on the "whole" woman, not just diet and nutrition. From work to stress to relationships, the Women in Wellness™ program understands that lasting wellness comes from a successful plan that integrates our many aspects. You can learn more about the program or enjoy a free month membership by logging on to www.womeninwellness.com

time and moon cycle. And I've tried diets where I've dealt meal cards; counted calories and leg lifts; measured points, inches, heart rates, circumferences and diameters. They've all lead me back to the same place. "Garbage in, garbage out. Unbalanced in, unbalanced out."

I'm happy to report that I am now a size 4 (don't hate me, it didn't come easily). That's not due to a naturally friendly metabolism, genes or luck. Quite the contrary, for 15 years I battled daily with the scale and for 10 years had an active and consuming eating disorder. My weight topped at 204 when I entered the hospital to deliver my first child. I figured my child would weigh at least 90 pounds. Imagine my surprise when I left a day later with an 8 pound baby girl—and only 15 pounds lighter. From there, I spent seven years testing the spectrum of tricks and diet devices. I tried mail order, phone order, ab rollers—you name it, I owned it. I bring this up only because so many women battle with their weight and, of course, we are also facing unprecedented weight problems with our children. It took me so many years of unhealthy behavior to realize how important health is and to find a way to truly live a healthy life. For those who are interested, I want to share the keys to my success and perhaps they can open the door to yours.

Hop over the hoopla, fads and miracle cures. Ignore the magazines that tell you how to lose seven pounds by Thursday yet advertise 10 ways to make a sinful chocolate cake on the opposite page. Let it all go. You don't need to try to live up to some standard set by the latest fashion or diet guru. At the end of the day, the person you account to is *you*.

Satisfy your soul... not your scale. You are the one who needs to be satisfied. When we struggle with our weight and diet, it's often our soul that needs nourishing just as much as our body. What are you missing within yourself? Make a list and a plan of action for replenishing your self and your soul, as well as your body.

Start with a healthy attitude before your healthy diet. So many times we enter diets or new eating plans at a point where we are frustrated or disgusted with ourselves. No wonder we can't "stick to the plan." How can we expect to meet our goals when our attitudes are negative or depressed? Before beginning a healthy program, begin with a healthy and positive attitude.

Gather some teammates. You have probably heard the saying, "It takes a village to raise a child." Consider yourself at the child stage of a health program. Just as you wouldn't leave a child alone in new territory, don't sentence yourself to struggle in silence. Find a support network to share your success. Support was vital for me in turning over a new leaf. It's important to have at least three people in your support network. (If you have only two, it's very easy for it to fizzle.) I did e-mail support with two other gals who sought a healthy life. When we had our tough times, we could find strength in each other and the knowledge that we weren't alone.

Set realistic goals. Another vital part of my success was due to a Personal Wellness Coach. I used Carrie Myers Smith, President of WomeninWellness.Com as a guide and sounding

BREAKFAST, AND DESSERT

You'll also notice that I have not included specific lunch or breakfast items. You'll be pleased to know that I am not so certifiably crazy that I believe one could prepare homemade breakfast, lunch and dinner daily! Since breakfast is usually rushed (if eaten at all) and lunch is normally had at work or school, it makes sense to focus on the dinnertime meal. However, as most studies show, going without breakfast is not a good idea. So I do address the topics of Rush Hour Breakfasts on page 27.

Lastly, I have not included desserts. While in my ideal world I would have dessert every night, if the mirror would allow it, such is not the case. One too many scoops of ice cream and the scale is quick to remind me of caloric law! I have included numerous Rush Hour Desserts in Chapter Nine—you can add these to your grocery list as you need them.

board. In our first session, I wanted goals like... workout seven days a week, eat five healthy dinners, etc. Carrie combated my obsessive personality and offered baby steps instead. We started with very obtainable goals. Exercise twice the first week. Eat two healthy dinners. All in all I had about five simple goals. By focusing only on those goals, I became successful. As my confidence grew, I could build on those goals.

Try an "at least" mentality. Many times I had tried to makeover my life in a day or with a New Year's resolution. I wanted to wake up and magically engage in healthy behavior. What a recipe for failure! I remember how brutal I was to myself when my plans crumbled as I passed a Danish. When I started the Women in Wellness program, I developed what I refer to as an "at least mentality". Two of my goals for the first week were to exercise twice and eat two healthy dinners. I decided that no matter what happened over the course of the week, I would "at least" complete those two challenges. Furthermore, I would be pleased, no matter what happened, as long as I completed the two challenges. If I ate ice cream nonstop in between, I would still be nice to myself. I would be pleased that I had met the two simple goals and would add additional goals each week. By doing this, I didn't have to give up and throw the baby out with the bathwater. Instead, I could increase my number of healthy behaviors over a period of time. As my healthy behaviors increased, there became less and less time for my destructive patterns. Eventually, the destructive patterns went away all on their own. The coolest part was, it didn't hurt! I didn't have any cravings. I didn't forbid anything. I simply focused on little healthy steps, two healthy steps at a time.

Erase excuses and energize your exercise. I don't love exercising, in fact, for most of my life I've detested it. I've tried step aerobics, Pilates, home workouts, group classes and many other scenarios, only to feel like participating was torture. When I finally realized it was a necessity to a healthy lifestyle I said, "Okay—then let's make it something good." I began to look for a program that matched my personality. I am competitive and like to measure my results. I found that running was a great source of exercise for me. Although I had never run more than a mile in my life and was sure I would hate it; I discovered I was wrong. I could compete in 5K's, 10K's or half-marathons and measure my progress and time. I could constantly push and improve to "beat my best." Granted, I'm not a great runner and I often walk/jog instead of run. My times are lousy by most people's standards—but I don't care. It's never been about "beating the world," it's about pushing me to be the "best me" I can be.

When I first started I couldn't walk 3 miles, let alone run them. Imagine when 4 months later I ran 13 miles. What a feeling! Sure, I was probably one of the last to finish—but that didn't matter—what did matter, was that I finished. When I relocated to the Midwest, running wasn't as pleasant in sub-zero temperatures. For the first time in my life, I enrolled in a martial arts class. Again, I could measure my progress by moving through the belt system. I've been involved in the martial arts for a year and just received my brown belt. I feel strong and comfortable in my body. The martial arts have become a lifeline for releasing stress and staying fit. In 2003 I have also set a goal to run, walk, jog or roll through my first marathon. (SIDE NOTE: I'm going to do the Chicago LaSalle Marathon in October 2003... if you want to join me, drop me an e-mail at brook@rushhourcook.com)

While stationary bicycling and step aerobics left me longing for a beach in Maui, I've finally found a program that matches what I need from exercise. So get creative and explore the options around you. I am convinced that there are enough exercises on this planet—from racquetball to spinning to tennis to aquatics to hiking—everyone can find something that matches their personality—it's just a matter of looking. Enough excuses.

SMART CHOICES

If you are health-conscious and trying to make better dietary choices, follow the guidelines below when preparing these recipes. I always follow them and doing so makes most of these recipes stay within the 30% or less fat guidelines.

Instead of...	Choose...
Regular Sour Cream	Low-fat or nonfat sour cream. When used in recipes, there is only a subtle difference.
Butter	Light whipped butter. (Stay away from margarine when possible—although low in fat it has many other ingredients which are bad news and outweigh the low-fat benefit.)
Cream Soups	Reduced-fat versions of these soups. However, if you are watching your sodium, make sure to check out the labels.
Ricotta Cheese	Fat-free ricotta cheese tastes almost the same as whole fat when incorporated into a recipe.
Yogurt	Choose the fat-free option,
Mayonnaise	Choose the fat-free option. If using for sandwiches, try other sauces instead like Honey-Dijon mustard or fat-free dressing.
Whipped Topping	The low-fat and fat-free options taste almost as good!
Cheese	Opt for reduced-fat cheese when incorporated into a recipe. However, if you are doing cheese and crackers, go with the real stuff. Low-fat and fat-free cheeses have a long way to go before catching up to the tasty, real stuff!
Milk	Try skim or fat-free. They take a while to get used to but are well worth the health benefit.
White bread	White bread has been called the natural-killer! It's filled with stuff that is bad news. Try a whole-wheat bread instead. When looking at the ingredients make sure it says WHOLE-WHEAT. Many times suppliers will say WHEAT or HONEY-WHEAT—but those are not true whole-wheat choices!
Ground beef	Always choose the leanest cut—94% fat-free is a good one or substitute extra-lean ground turkey.

CHAPTER THREE

A BALANCED BREAKFAST

I n today's world we are lucky to even have breakfast—let alone a healthy, balanced one! Yet the statistics keep reminding us that breakfast is the most important meal of the day. While I often neglected breakfast as a meal, once I had my daughter I knew it was time to take breakfast seriously.

As someone who often suffered afternoon "lag times" and carbo cravings, I learned that choosing a high protein breakfast minimized both.

To make breakfast speedy yet nutritious, I've found it easiest to choose a few favorites and rotate week to week. In our home, cereal is a definite favorite. Where else can you get a zillion vitamins in a one-cup serving? We each have 2-3 mostly-healthy cereals for rushed mornings. To increase nutrition value, slice a banana or add berries. Compliment that with a glass of orange juice and a multi-vitamin and the day is off to a winning start. Here are some of my other favorite quick and easy breakfasts:

THE RUSH HOUR COOK'S MORNING SMOOTHIE

Until my "healthy life makeover" I had never eaten breakfast. The key to my consuming this all-important meal was in finding this quick, high-protein solution that I can eat on the run:

1 cup frozen berries of your choice
½ frozen banana (peel bananas, split in half, wrap in foil and freeze. This is a great way to use brown bananas. They still taste great in a smoothie!
½ cup nonfat plain yogurt
½ cup orange juice (more or less depending on the consistency you like)
2 tablespoons flax seed*
1 tablespoon organic greens*
1 scoop whey protein powder (vanilla flavored)*

Combine all ingredients in a blender and mix well.

These ingredients can be purchased at health supply stores and GNC® www.gnc.com They are all optional ingredients.

FOR MORE SMOOTHIE RECIPES, SEE PAGE 54.

This is a great morning snack for kids, too! They taste so rich and creamy—it's like having a delicious berry shake!

- ☐ English muffin with strawberry jam
- ☐ One egg, poached on a slice of whole wheat toast (try poaching your eggs in the microwave!)
- ☐ A scrambled egg with melted cheese, mushrooms and onions
- ☐ Whole wheat toast with a light dusting of butter, sugar and cinnamon
- ☐ Toast with peanut butter and banana
- ☐ Slice of cantaloupe, honeydew or other fresh fruit
- ☐ Granola topped with vanilla yogurt and sliced fruit
- ☐ The Rush Hour Smoothie (on previous page)
- ☐ Oatmeal or other hot cereal
- ☐ Cottage cheese and half a whole-wheat bagel
- ☐ Half a toasted whole-wheat English muffin topped with two slices of turkey bacon and melted cheese

My daughter on the other hand hates English muffins and believes eggs are "disgusting." Her list looks something like this...

- ☐ Toast, with crusts cut off, and jelly
- ☐ Yogurt (any flavor...bonus if it comes in a tube!)
- ☐ Fresh fruit
- ☐ Granola Bar
- ☐ Pancake, waffle or other syrup covered item (See homemade-alternatives note below.)
- ☐ Muffins (Another good option to make-ahead and freeze.)

To keep it easy, I choose two breakfasts for each week and alternate them daily.

HOMEMADE ALTERNATIVES

One time I purchased a package of waffles that looked incredibly delicious in the deli. I then forgot about them. Two months later, when I looked in my pantry I discovered they were still there—in perfect form. I can only imagine the preservatives! I vowed never to buy another box. Make your own healthy and quick waffles, pancakes or French toast from scratch and cook up some extra. Freeze in individual zip-top freezer bags for quick and easy breakfasts or snacks. To reheat, simply pop in the toaster. There is a Perfectly Pleasing Pancake recipe on page 39.

CHAPTER FOUR

TEN DAZZLING DRESSINGS AND MARVELOUS MARINADES

The "Simple Salad" (see page 64) is a mainstay in this book. With all the dressing combinations listed here, plus those you devise on your own, the Simple Salad offers a vast array of possibilities!

Forget the store-bought bottled choices—dressings are easy to make and tasty as well! (Not to mention, homemade dressings are a great way to impress your friends.) Try these Top Ten Dazzling Dressings…

1. ORANGE-DIJON DRESSING

½ cup orange juice
¼ cup Dijon-style mustard

½ cup white wine vinegar
2 tablespoons olive oil

Whisk all ingredients together. Store for up to 7 days in refrigerator. Makes 8 servings.

2. SUPER-CITRUS DRESSING

1 cup honey
1½ cups Dijon-style mustard

1 cup orange juice

Whisk ingredients together. Store in refrigerator for up to 1 week. Makes 10 servings.

3. CREAMY GARLIC & CHIVE DRESSING

20 garlic cloves, peeled   1 cup ricotta cheese
½ cup yogurt   ¼ cup chopped chives
1 teaspoon salt   ½ teaspoon black pepper
1 cup water

Combine garlic and water; bring to a boil. Simmer 10 minutes. Remove garlic and place in blender along with 2 tablespoons of the cooking liquid. Add ricotta cheese and yogurt to blender and purée until smooth.
Stir in chives, salt and pepper.
Cover and refrigerate for at least
2 hours prior to serving. Makes 8
servings.
.

4. CREAMY ITALIAN DRESSING

1 cup mayonnaise, low-fat
2 tablespoons grated Parmesan cheese
2 tablespoons red wine vinegar
2 teaspoons sugar
1 teaspoon Italian seasoning
½ teaspoon salt
½ teaspoon garlic pepper
3-4 tablespoons milk

Combine all ingredients except milk. Chill for a minimum of two hours. Add milk to create desired consistency. Makes 12 servings.

5. CREAMY BUTTERMILK DRESSING

½ cup buttermilk   ½ cup mayonnaise
2 teaspoons Dijon-style mustard   1 clove garlic, minced

Combine all ingredients except milk. Chill for a minimum of two hours. Add milk to create desired consistency. Makes 12 servings.

6. SWEET & SOUR DRESSING

2 tablespoons honey
2 teaspoons Dijon-style mustard
½ cup unsweetened apple juice
Salt and pepper to taste

Blend ingredients. Salt and pepper to taste. Makes 8 servings.

7. FRESH & FRUITY DRESSING

4 tablespoons lemon juice
4 tablespoons unsweetened apple juice
2 tablespoons olive oil
2 cloves garlic, minced
Salt and pepper to taste

Blend ingredients. Salt and pepper to taste. Makes 8 servings.

8. LEMON-GARLIC VINAIGRETTE*

¼ teaspoon dry mustard
⅓ cup extra-virgin olive oil
2 tablespoons lemon juice
2 tablespoons red wine vinegar
1 clove minced garlic
Place all ingredients in a jar and shake well. Makes 8 servings.

9. BALSAMIC VINAIGRETTE*

½ cup balsamic vinegar
⅓ cup extra-virgin olive oil
1 tablespoon sugar
Place all ingredients in a jar or blender and shake well. Makes 5 servings.

10. SMOKEY-TOMATO DRESSING*

1 large tomato
1½ teaspoons Liquid Smoke
2 cloves garlic, minced
1½ cups mayonnaise
¼ teaspoon salt
2 tablespoons olive oil
1-2 tablespoons sugar
1 teaspoon chopped capers
1½ tablespoons minced parsley
In a bowl mix 1 large tomato (that has been peeled, halved, juices squeezed out and finely diced) with the remaining ingredients. Makes 6 servings.

*Excerpted from Cooking for Blondes: gourmet recipes for the culinarily challenged by Rhonda Levitch. www.cookingforblondes.net

MARINADE MADNESS

Looking for creative flairs for routine dishes? Try these marinades on your meats for added fun and flavor.

ROSEMARY-BASIL MARINADE

¼ cup olive oil
5 sprigs, fresh rosemary
2 teaspoons dried basil
1 lemon, quartered
Pour olive oil into shallow dish. Squeeze lemon juice into oil and then drop in lemon peels. Add basil and rosemary and meat of choice. Cover and marinate up to 6 hours.

ITALIAN MARINADE

1 cup bottled Italian dressing
1 cup Dijon-style mustard
Mix both ingredients. Add meat and marinate up to 4 hours.

WHITE WINE MARINADE

1 cup dry white wine
½ cup Dijon-style mustard
1 tablespoon marjoram
1 tablespoon olive oil
Mix all ingredients. Immerse meat. Marinate up to 6 hours.

RED WINE MARINADE

1 cup red wine
3 tablespoons Worcestershire sauce
1 teaspoon cracked black pepper
1 tablespoon olive oil
3 minced garlic cloves
Mix all ingredients. Immerse meat. Marinate up to 6 hours.

NOTE: Best to marinate in refrigerator. Discard any leftover marinades if not using directly in cooking process.

CHAPTER FIVE
STOCKING UP ON SNACKS

M any of our kids today live primarily on snacks. They have snacks when they come home from school and often snack their way through dinner if we are not around to provide a home-cooked alternative. Keeping a good stock of snacks becomes vitally important to maintaining our children's health. After all, a child will only be able to choose from the options we provide them. Although Oreos® and Fritos® might be the quickest and simplest solutions, they certainly aren't the healthiest. Try some of these healthy snacks to tide your youngster over.

- Microwave popcorn (low in fat and filling to prevent overindulging in non-nutritious snacks)
- Nuts
- Granola, Nutri-Grain® or other cereal bars
- Trail mix, preferably homemade
- Yogurt (any shape, size or flavor)
- Soft pretzels (I could live off of these and with only 1 gram of fat each, they are easy to indulge in!)
- Soft tortillas with simple fillings like lean ham and cheese
- Frozen homemade soups that can be zapped in the microwave for a quick, warm snack
- Hard boiled eggs
- Celery and carrot sticks, sliced and rinsed, with a container of fat-free ranch dressing nearby
- Rykrisp® or Melba® crackers with cheese
- Sliced apple with peanut butter

While overhauling your snack supply, it may be a good time to overhaul some eating rules, too. When we moved into our new home, we added a "no grazing rule." The rule applied to all of us, since we all had the habit of grabbing some unhealthy snack and having it virtually disappear while we minded the television, computer or some other activity. Our new rule allows us only to eat when seated at the table or kitchen island. It's amazing how much less we eat! Eating and grazing can become so habitual you almost forget you are doing it!

In addition to the convenient snacks on the previous page, here are a few that can be prepared in a flash!

PITA CRISPS

3 (6-inch) pita breads | 3 tablespoons olive oil
Salt and pepper to taste | Garlic, minced (if desired)
Salsa or dip for serving, (optional)

Cut pitas into single-layer triangles and arrange on cookie sheet, being careful not to overlap. Each pita should be cut into 8 triangles. Brush with oil. Sprinkle with salt, pepper and garlic according to taste. Broil until lightly browned. Serve with a dip or salsa on the side, if desired. Makes 4 servings of 6 triangles each. (You can get creative here and top with cheeses, veggies, etc.—there is also a Cinnamon Chip recipe on the following p-age.)

BERRY-GOOD FRUIT PARFAITS

1 package raspberry gelatin | 2 cups blueberries
2 cups sliced strawberries | 1¾ cups milk
1 package vanilla instant pudding

Prepare raspberry gelatin according to package directions but instead of pouring into a bowl, pour into 8 parfait or other tall glasses and refrigerate till firm. Top with ½ of the fruit. Make pudding according to package directions and scoop over fruit. Top with other ½ of fruit. Cover and refrigerate for 45 minutes prior to serving.

BROILED MELBAS

1 cup light mayonnaise
1 cup freshly grated
  Parmesan cheese
1 teaspoon parsley
30 melba round crackers

Combine mayonnaise and Parmesan cheese. Add parsley and stir. Spread a teaspoon onto each melba round and broil on a cookie sheet until golden brown (1-2 minutes). There is plenty of room for variation in this recipe. Be creative when choosing your toppings. Makes 30 melba treats.

CINNAMON CHIPS

Not the healthiest choice on the block, but a great indulgence for a sweet tooth instead of cookies, cakes, etc.

6 flour tortillas (I usually use whole wheat)
5 tablespoons melted butter
Cinnamon and sugar

Cut flour tortillas into 8 pieces, making triangular chips. Spread chips on a cookie sheet in a single layer. Drizzle butter evenly over chips. Sprinkle with cinnamon and sugar. Bake in a 350-degree oven for 10-12 minutes. Let cool and then transfer to bowl. Makes 6 servings.

CHAPTER SIX

THE ART OF BULK COOKING

I f you are looking for a way to revolutionize the way you cook, consider bulk cooking for the freezer. One of our company's best-selling authors, Deborah Taylor-Hough has taken this cooking method and made it into an exact science, allowing families throughout the world to spend less time in the kitchen and more time at the family table. Here are a few tips on how you, too, can enjoy this method!

Deborah advises that you sit down with a blank calendar and choose your recipes for 30 days. Consider how many times your family will eat the same meal twice. For example, can you get away with serving lasagna 3 times in 30 days? If so, pencil it in. Once you have all your recipes written in, create a master list of ingredients. Use that as your shopping list. Do all your prep-work (cutting, dicing, etc.) for all the recipes the night before your big cooking day. Then, move through the process of preparing and packaging all the meals on the following day. As you complete each recipe, use a black permanent marker to write the date frozen and any additional preparation-needs. For example, "Top with 1 cup cheese and bake for 40 minutes at 350 degrees." This will make it easier for others to finish preparing the meals when you are unavailable. Tuck your meals in the freezer and you're well-stocked for the month!

There is an art to bulk-freezer cooking, so if it is really of interest to you, I encourage you to pick up *Frozen Assets: how to cook for a day and eat for a month* (ISBN 1-891400-61-4) or *Frozen Assets Lite and Easy* (ISBN 1-891400-28-2) or *Frozen Assets Readers' Favorites* (1-891400-185).Deborah shows you how to cook the meals partially before freezing and then complete the cooking process when you reheat the meal—avoiding that leftover-taste that scares most people from this cooking method. In any event, here is one great, versatile recipe excerpted from her book *Frozen Assets,* (www.championpress.com):

BEEF MIX

The versatile recipe below gives you everything you need to prepare 3 meatloaves, 1 Salisbury steak meal and 3 meals of meatballs (to use with pasta sauces, meatball sandwiches, etc.)

24 ounces tomato sauce
3 cups dry bread crumbs
7 eggs, lightly beaten
1 cup onion, finely chopped
½ green pepper, finely chopped
2 teaspoons salt (optional)
¼ teaspoon dried thyme, crushed
¼ teaspoon dried marjoram, crushed
8 pounds ground beef

Combine first eight ingredients. Add ground beef and mix well. Divide meat mixture in half.

For Meatloaf:
Shape ½ mixture into three loaves and place in a high-sided baking dish. Don't allow the loaves to touch. Bake at 350 degrees for one hour. Cool. Wrap in heavy-duty foil, label and freeze. To serve, thaw loaves and bake in 350-degree oven for 30 minutes or until heated through.

For Meatballs:
Shape into meatballs and place on broiler pan so grease can drain while cooking. Bake uncovered in a 350-degree oven for 30 minutes. Divide into meal-sized portions. To prevent meatballs from freezing into a solid meatball-mass, freeze individually on cookie sheets and then place in freezer bags. Label and freeze. To serve, thaw and reheat with your choice of sauces.

For Salisbury Steak:
Form remaining meat mixture into oval ½-inch thick patties.
Heat oil in nonstick skillet over medium heat until hot. Place
beef patties in skillet; cook seven to eight minutes or until
centers are no longer pink, turning once. Cool, place in freezer
bags; freeze. To serve, thaw and heat with 1 (10.75 ounce) can
of cream of mushroom soup poured over as sauce. Serve with
rice or noodles.

PERFECTLY PLEASING PANCAKES

H ere is another great recipe to double or triple for a quick
breakfast. Just toss an individually frozen pancake in the
toaster to have a homemade meal.

4 eggs
1 quart milk
3 tablespoons vanilla extract
4 tablespoons melted butter
4 cups flour
¼ cup sugar
¼ cup baking powder
2 teaspoons salt
¾ cup vegetable oil
Butter (or cooking spray)

In a large bowl, beat eggs; add milk and vanilla and mix well.
Add melted butter and stir. Add dry ingredients and oil, mix
well. Heat griddle or frying pan to medium. Melt a tad of
butter in the pan (or use cooking spray). Ladle pancake batter
onto griddle or pan by the spoonful. Brown lightly on each
side. Makes 6 servings.

To Freeze:
Store cooked pancakes in individual freezer bags.

To Serve:
Place frozen pancakes in toaster and toast on medium setting.
Serve with butter and syrup or fruit preserves.

CHAPTER SEVEN

PRACTICALLY INSTANT FAMILY DINNERS (JUST ADD FAMILY)

The key to the recipes here is speed. They are far from gourmet fare—but they are better than a trip to the local fast food joint! These recipes define quick, simple and easy. Choose one or two and keep the ingredients on hand for "crunch-nights".

TOAST-BURGERS

1 piece bread (per person)
1 (3 ounce) lean hamburger patty (per person)
1 (10.5 ounce) can condensed cream of mushroom soup

Toast bread. Cook hamburger patty for 3-5 minutes per side or until beef is browned and cooked through. Place beef patty on top of toast. Heat soup over medium heat, adding just enough liquid to make a thick sauce. Pour warmed soup over beef and serve "open-faced".

SHAKE IT & BAKE IT!

As stated earlier, this is not a section devoted to health! That being said, Shake-N-Bake® remains one of my all-time "make it quick" solutions. Keep a couple bags on hand along with chicken breasts or pork chops. About an hour before dinner, shake and bake your meat of choice and throw some baked potatoes in the oven. A healthier alternative to Shake-N-Bake® are bread crumbs. Experiment with the many flavors available—from Italian to Garlic & Herb to Plain. Lightly coat meat with water and then dredge into bread crumbs. For a bit of variation and extra flavor, moisten with egg instead of water. You can also moisten with mustard, soy-sauce or any liquid that will allow bread crumbs to adhere to meat.

SALS-A-RONI

16 ounces elbow macaroni   1 pound ground beef
16 ounces salsa   10 ounces Cheddar cheese

Cook macaroni according to package directions. Brown beef in skillet. Drain. Mix salsa and cheese in a microwave-safe bowl and heat for 2 minutes. Mix all ingredients together in a baking dish and heat in a 350-degree oven for 20-30 minutes. Come on... we're aiming for quick and edible, right? Give it a try! Makes 4-6 servings.

INSTANT TACOS

Refried beans (warmed) or pre-cooked ground beef
Shredded cheese (your choice)
Flour tortillas
Sour cream (optional)
Salsa (optional)

BEAN-VERSION: Spread warmed refried beans over a small flour tortilla and sprinkle with shredded cheese. Fold and then top with salsa and sour cream.

BEAN-LESS VERSION: Prepare ground beef with a packet of taco seasoning (following directions on seasoning packet). Store beef in single-serving amounts in freezer bags, To prepare an instant taco, defrost and heat meat in microwave. Substitute the beef for beans
in the above instructions.

ITALIAN PASTA SKILLET

3 packages of Ramen™ noodles, beef flavor
1 pound ground round
20 ounces diced tomatoes, undrained
1 cup water
1½ cups mozzarella cheese, shredded

Brown beef over medium heat. Drain. Add tomatoes, water and 1 Ramen™ seasoning packet (save the other two for another recipe) and heat to boiling. Mix in noodles from all 3 packets. Cook 5 minutes or until noodles are tender. Scoop onto plates and top with cheese. Makes 6 servings.

CHICKEN AND RAVIOLI

1 pound pre-cooked chicken breast strips (such as Louis Rich™)
¾ cup chicken broth
9 ounces refrigerated ravioli
Parmesan cheese

Place broth and ravioli in skillet and heat to boiling. Cover and reduce heat, simmering for 3-5 minutes or until ravioli are tender. Add chicken and heat through. Serve onto plates and top with Parmesan cheese, if desired. Makes 4 servings.

GENERIC PIZZA

English muffins, halved (one half per person), or pita bread
Tomato sauce
Part-skim mozzarella cheese, shredded
Fresh veggies (green peppers, mushrooms, onions and any
   other veggies you like!)

For a speedy lunch, cover a toasted English muffin-half or
mini pita with tomato sauce, shredded part-skim mozzarella
cheese and veggies. Broil just until cheese is melted.

*Kids often like theirs without the veggies! If
that's the case, serve carrots on the side with
ranch dressing, or serve celery and peanut
butter.*

FRENCH DIPS

1 pound deli roast-beef, shredded
1 packet au-jus gravy mix
4 hoagie rolls (split, butter and toast until golden)

Spray a nonstick skillet with cooking spray. Mix au-jus in a
small sauce pan over low-heat. Place beef in skillet and add ¼
cup of the au-jus. Warm meat and pile onto hoagie rolls. Place
remaining au-jus in shallow bowls and serve along side
sandwiches for dipping. Makes 4 servings.

BREAKFAST FOR DINNER

Scrambled eggs and toast are a great meal that we rarely have
time to enjoy during our rush hour mornings! Try breakfast
for dinner for a quick solution to "What's for dinner?"
Pancakes, French toast and omelets are other morning-
favorites that we can enjoy at dinner time, too!

CHAPTER EIGHT

STEAMING SUCCESS

Despite my firm belief that there should be a few basic rules about cooking—like universal cook times for each major food group—each food does have its own needs for maximum taste.

The guide below can help you when trying to optimally steam your vegetables for both taste and nutrition. If steaming more than one vegetable on the list, start with the one that takes the most time and then add the others at applicable intervals. P.S. If you are reading this give yourself a gold star, steaming your vegetables remains the healthiest way to cook veggies while retaining maximum nutrients.

Artichoke (whole)	40-45 minutes
Green Beans	4-5 minutes
Beets	30-35 minutes
Broccoli with Stalk	15-20 minutes
Broccoli Florets	5-7 minutes
Cabbage (cut into wedges)	6 minutes
Carrots (¼ inch thick)	6-8 minutes
Cauliflower florets	4-6 minutes
Cauliflower (head)	12-16 minutes
Celery	15 minutes
Corn on the Cob	5-8 minutes
Peas	2-3 minutes
Peppers	30 minutes
Onions	25 minutes
Potatoes (cut into 2-inch pieces)	15 minutes
Spinach	4-5 minutes
Sweet Potatoes (whole)	40-45 minutes
Tomatoes	12 minutes
Winter squash (2-inch pieces)	15-20 minutes
Zucchini (¼-inch slices)	6-8 minutes

It's Not Enough to Eat Your Veggies....

You have to eat them right! Avoid these common mistakes in order to maximize nutrient intake...

☐ Do not place vegetables in water until after it is boiling. The greater the time spent in the water, the less the nutrient retention.

☐ When possible, leave skins on while cooking. More nutrients are lost via the exposed surface.

☐ Steaming is still the best cooking method for preparing your vegetables. (See chart on previous page.)

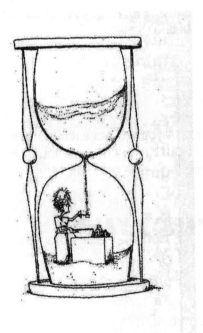

CHAPTER NINE

DAZZLING DESSERTS

As mentioned in the introduction of this book, although I love desserts I know it is not practical to have them every day! For that reason I did not include desserts in the weekly menus. However, on these pages I have included some wonderful delights that follow the Rush Hour™ Rules. On the nights you choose to have dessert, I truly hope that you'll enjoy these!

MINUTE MERINGUE DESSERT

6 store-bought baked meringues (unless you're Martha—then bake them yourself. Of course, if you're Martha, you probably aren't reading this book.)
3 cups chocolate, vanilla or strawberry frozen-nonfat yogurt
1½ cups strawberries, sliced
Chocolate syrup
Whipped topping

Scoop ½ cup of frozen yogurt into each meringue. Top with ¼ cup strawberries, 1 tablespoon of chocolate syrup and a dollop of whipped topping. Makes 6 servings.

QUICK CHERRY TARTS

1 tube refrigerated crescent rolls
¼ cup powdered sugar
3 ounces cream cheese, softened
1 cup cherry pie filling
Vanilla ice cream (optional)

Roll out dough. Cut into 2-inch circles. Place dough in muffin cups. Beat cream cheese and sugar in a small bowl until smooth. Divvy up cream cheese mixture between muffin tins. Top with cherry pie filling. Bake for 12-15 minutes in a 375-degree oven. Top with vanilla ice cream, if desired. Makes 6-8 servings.

BANANARAMA CREAM PIE

1 (6 ounce) ready-made graham cracker crust
1 small package vanilla instant pudding
1⅓ cups milk
1 (8 ounce) tub of whipped topping
2 medium sliced bananas

Make pudding using 1⅓ cup cold milk. Spread ½ cup of the whipped topping on the bottom of the crust. Place one banana's worth of slices over the whipped topping. Layer on pudding and place the other sliced banana over the pudding. Top with additional whipped topping, covering the banana layer completely. Chill until set (1 hour minimum). Makes 8 servings.

CRISPY PEANUT BUTTER CHOCOLATE PIE

¼ cup creamy peanut butter
1 tablespoon butter
1½ cups Rice Krispie™ cereal
1 package of chocolate fudge instant pudding
1⅓ cups milk
1 (8 ounce) tub of whipped topping
½ cup of Reeses Pieces™

Put butter and peanut butter in microwave safe-bowl. Heat until melted, then stir in the cereal. Pour into bottom of greased pie pan and press down to form "crust." (Note: you can use wax paper or a wooden spoon to make spreading easier.) Make pudding according to pie filling directions on package. Fold one cup of the whipped topping into the pudding. Pour into the "crust". Top with the remaining whipped topping and garnish with Reeses Pieces™. Chill for 2 hours before serving. Makes 8 servings.

HOT FUDGE MOCHA SHAKE

4 cups mocha ice cream
½ cup hot fudge topping
1 cup milk

Put all ingredients in a blender and mix on high for one minute or until desired consistency. Pour into tall glasses. Serve with a spoon and enjoy! Makes 4 servings.

FOR COFFEE LOVERS: Add 1 tablespoon instant coffee to the mix before blending.

FOR NON-COFFEE LOVERS: Substitute vanilla ice cream for mocha ice cream.

FRUIT PIZZA

1 tube refrigerated sugar cookie dough
1 container strawberry cream cheese fruit dip
2 cups assorted fresh fruit (grapes, kiwi, strawberries
   raspberries, blueberries, cherries)

Roll out cookie dough to fit pizza pan. Bake at 375 degrees for 12-15 minutes until golden brown. Cool. Spread fruit dip on top of cookie dough and top with sliced fresh fruit. Slice and serve. Makes 8 servings.

Careful, this can be addictive! (And no, having a whole pie does not count as your five fruit servings!) You can also make a frosting with cream cheese and sugar. Mix cream cheese in a small mixing bowl adding sugar until desired sweetness is achieved. Spread in place of strawberry cream cheese in above recipe.

FONDUE FOR YOU

1 (14-ounce) can condensed milk
1 cup semisweet chocolate chips
Milk, as needed

Combine condensed milk and chocolate over low heat until melted. Keep warm for dipping. Thin to desired consistency with milk—as needed.

Serve with:
Strawberries
Graham Crackers
Bananas
Brownies
Marshmallows
Cantaloupe
Angel food cake
Lady fingers

VANILLA BERRY DREAM

1 package instant vanilla pudding
2 cups cold milk
2 cups fresh berries (raspberries, blueberries,
   strawberries—use a combination for maximum flavor)
Whipped topping

Mix pudding with milk in bowl. Beat with wire whisk for 2-3 minutes. Pour into dessert bowls. Refrigerate for at least 30 minutes. Top with berries and whipped topping. Serve well-chilled. Makes 4-6 servings.

SIMPLE STRAWBERRY SHORTCAKE

1 angel food cake cut into 8 pieces
1 (16 ounce) package fresh strawberries
½ cup sugar
Whipped topping

Wash and hull strawberries (or if you are like me, just cut the tops off) then slice. Mix strawberries with sugar. Cover and refrigerate for at least two hours. Mix once while chilling. Place strawberries and the sugary juice from the strawberries on top of the angle food cake. Top with whipped topping. Makes 8 servings.

CHOCOLATE LOVERS: Drizzle chocolate syrup over the top!

....
: Slice strawberries in a snap with an egg dicer!   :
....

SNICKER® BAR SURPRISE

2 Snickers® Candy Bars sliced into ½-inch pieces
2 sliced red delicious apples
2 sliced green apples
1 (12 ounce) container whipped topping
Cocktail peanuts
Chocolate and caramel sauce (optional)

Combine Snickers®, apples and two-thirds of whipped topping in a serving bowl. Top with remaining whipped topping. Sprinkle with cocktail peanuts and drizzle with chocolate and caramel sauce if desired. Makes 8 servings. (Warning: this is another addictive combination!)

CRISPY CINNAMON SUNDAE

2 tablespoons sugar
2 teaspoons cinnamon
3 fat-free flour tortillas, cut into wedges
2 tablespoons melted butter
⅓ cup caramel topping, heated
3 cups vanilla ice cream

Combine sugar and cinnamon. Brush both sides of tortilla wedges with melted butter and then sprinkle with sugar mixture. Place wedges on a baking sheet. Broil for one or two minutes to brown lightly. Melt caramel topping according to directions. Place ½ cup ice cream into a dessert bowl. Drizzle caramel topping over ice cream. Surround ice cream with the cinnamon tortilla crisps.

DARLENE'S 5 MINUTE FUDGE

⅔ cup Carnation® milk
1⅔ cups sugar
½ teaspoon salt
1½ cups miniature marshmallows
1½ cups semisweet chocolate chips
1 teaspoon vanilla

Over medium heat bring milk, sugar and salt to a boil. Cook 5 minutes, stirring constantly. Remove from heat. Add in miniature marshmallows, chocolate chips and vanilla. Stir until marshmallows melt and fudge is smooth, about 1 minute. Pour into buttered 8-inch square pan. Cool. Cut into 1-inch squares. Makes 64 candies. Store in airtight container.

To Freeze:
Store squares between layers of waxed paper in an airtight container. Keeps for 1 month.

BANANAS FOSTER

⅓ cup pineapple juice
3 tablespoons dark rum
2 medium bananas, peeled and halved
1 tablespoon, plus 1 teaspoon firmly packed dark brown sugar
2 tablespoons water

In medium skillet, combine pineapple juice, rum, sugar and 2 tablespoons water; bring mixture to a boil over medium-high heat. Reduce heat to low; simmer about five minutes. Add bananas to mixture and cook one more minute. Serve warm.

Kids probably wont like the rum in this recipe, but it's simply too good to omit from the book! Try a simple banana split for the little ones with sliced bananas, vanilla ice cream and chocolate sauce.

Serving Suggestions:
☐ Serve warm on a dessert plate, topped with a dollop of sour cream or yogurt.
☐ Serve warm, rolled into crepes, topped with whipped cream or sour cream.
☐ Serve in the traditional fashion, over vanilla ice cream.

ANY-BERRY SAUCE

4 cups fresh berries (raspberries, blackberries, blueberries, strawberries)
½ cup granulated sugar

Combine ingredients in a saucepan over low heat until well-blended. If you like a thicker sauce, add up to 2 tablespoons of cornstarch. If using a seeded fruit, force sauce through a fine mesh sieve to remove seeds, then cool. Freeze for up to 6 months. This is a great recipe to preserve freshly-picked berries. To serve, simply leave sauce in refrigerator overnight. Serve over vanilla custard.

ALMOND BITES

¾ stick butter
¼ cup light brown sugar
1 cup flour
¼ cup almonds, finely chopped
¼ teaspoon salt

Beat butter and sugar till light and fluffy. Sift in flour and stir in almonds. Form dough into a 10-inch roll. Wrap in aluminum foil or wax paper and chill for 20 minutes. Cut roll in ¼-inch thick slices. Place on a greased cookie sheet in a 325-degree oven for 15-20 minutes. Makes 18-20 cookies.

SHOOTING STARS

1 cup flour
¾ stick butter
12 chocolate stars
1 tablespoon cocoa powder
2 tablespoons syrup

Sift flour and cocoa into a bowl. Beat butter with syrup until smooth and well-blended. Blend two mixtures together. Form into 1-inch circles and place on greased cookie sheet. Bake for 8-10 minutes or until done. Upon removing from oven, gently press a chocolate star into center of each cookie. Cool. Makes 1 dozen.

SOOTHING SMOOTHIES

When you need a refreshing treat nothing can take the place of a smoothie! I love these combos! With their delicious taste it's hard to believe they are low-fat and good for you, too! Encourage kids to try smoothie combos and let the sky be the limit. You may also want to check out www.planetsmoothie.com, they sell supplemental powders that can be incorporated into smoothies such as immune blast, energy enhancer, mood balancer and more! Grab a handful of these and you can have a "moody smoothie bar"!

ORANGE FROSTY

1 cup milk
1 cup water
1 can frozen orange juice concentrate
10 ice cubes
¼ cup sugar
1½ teaspoons vanilla

Mix in blender until smooth and foamy. Serve. Garnish with a sliced orange twist or a cherry.

BERRY SURPRISE

1 cup raspberry yogurt (use nonfat)
1 cup milk (use nonfat)
1 tablespoon confectioners' sugar
1 (16 ounce) bag of frozen mixed berries
Mix all ingredients in a blender until smooth.

Don't forget to try my personal favorite morning smoothie on page 27.

BODACIOUS BANANA AND BLUEBERRY SMOOTHIE

1 banana, peeled and frozen
¼ cup frozen blueberries
1 cup orange juice
⅓ cup vanilla low-fat yogurt
Toss all ingredients in a blender, mix and enjoy!

COFFEE-NANA SMOOTHIE

1 banana, peeled and frozen
¾ cup fat-free milk
1 (4-ounce) container low-fat coffee yogurt
Cinnamon
Banana slices, for garnish
Mix first three ingredients in a blender until well-blended.
Pour into serving glass. Top with freshly sliced bananas and a dusting of cinnamon.

HEATLHY SMOOTHIE

1 cup cherry juice
8 ounces fat-free vanilla yogurt
1 cup frozen raspberries
½ cup red seedless grapes
2 packets Stevia® sweetener
Mix all ingredients in a blender until well-blended. Pour into serving glasses. Garnish with a cherry, if desired.

ANOTHER FRUIT SMOOTHIE

1 kiwi fruit, peeled
¼ cantaloupe
1 ripe banana
1 cup mixed berry juice
Handful of ice cubes
Mix all ingredients and enjoy!

INSTANT O.J. SMOOTHIE

1 cup orange juice
1 cup frozen strawberries
1 banana, peeled and unfrozen
1 banana, peeled and frozen
Mix all ingredients in a blender, pour into serving glass and enjoy!

CHOCOLATE BANANA SMOOTHIE

1 banana, peeled and frozen
1 tablespoon cocoa powder
2 cups skim milk
2–3 tablespoons crunchy peanut butter
1½ tablespoons sugar (or to taste)
3 pecans
Handful of ice
Place all ingredients in a blender, mix well and enjoy!

JUST-LIKE-FRAP SMOOTHIE

¾ cup cold double-strength coffee
1 cup milk
2 cups ice cubes
3 tablespoons sugar
Place all ingredients in a blender, mix well and enjoy!

WATERMELON WONDER

4 cups cubed seeded watermelon
⅛ cup sifted powdered sugar
3 ounces frozen lemonade concentrate, thawed
Place all ingredients in a blender, mix well and enjoy!

2.

THE

RUSH HOUR

RECIPES

QUICK AND CRISPY CHICKEN
MASH-IT POTATOES

o

HAM AND SWISS PIZZA
FRUIT SALAD

o

EASY PASTA TOSS
CHOOSE-A-WAY BREADSTICKS

o

"PITA SOUP" AND CALZONE SANDWICH

o

FEISTY FIESTA CASSEROLE
SIMPLE SALAD
FRENCH BREAD

QUICK AND CRISPY CHICKEN

6 boneless, skinless chicken breasts
4 tablespoons flour
½ cup Dijon-style mustard
½ cup dry bread crumbs

Rinse chicken and pat dry. Coat chicken with flour, then spread with mustard and dredge in bread crumbs. Warm a skillet over medium heat and spray with cooking spray. Cook chicken for 5 to 6 minutes per side or until no longer pink. Serve with Mash-It Garlic Potatoes (below). Makes 6 servings.

MASH-IT GARLIC POTATOES

5 large baking potatoes
3 tablespoons butter
½ cup sour cream
2 tablespoons minced garlic
⅛ teaspoon salt
½ cup milk, more or less depending on your preference

Bring several quarts of water to boil in a Dutch oven or other large pot. Wash potatoes thoroughly. Peel and cut into quarters (leave skins on if you like) and cook for 10-15 minutes or until tender. Drain and transfer potatoes to mixing bowl. Add remaining ingredients and mix to desired consistency with an electric mixer. Makes 6 servings.

RUSH HOUR TIP

Try using buttermilk in place of regular milk for incredible flavor. For extra fluff, add a pinch of baking powder.

HAM AND SWISS PIZZA

1 (12-inch) Italian bread shell
6 ounces lean ham, diced
1¼ cups Swiss cheese, shredded
½ teaspoon dried parsley

Spread ham over pizza shell and top with cheese. Sprinkle
with parsley. Bake in a 400-degree oven for 10 minutes or
until cheese is melted. OPTIONAL: If you would like to add a
sauce, try Five Brothers® Light Alfredo Sauce. Put the sauce
on before the ham and cheese. Serve with a fresh fruit salad.
Makes 6 servings.

EASY PASTA TOSS

16 ounces linguine noodles
½ cup butter
3 tablespoons fresh parsley, chopped
⅛ cup Dijon-style mustard
2 tablespoons lemon juice
3 cloves garlic, minced
Salt and pepper to taste

Prepare pasta according to package directions. Drain and
reserve, keeping warm. Melt butter in a pan over medium
heat. Stir in parsley, mustard, lemon juice and garlic. Heat for
2-3 minutes. Toss sauce with pasta and then salt and pepper
to taste. Serve with Choose-A-Way Breadsticks, see recipe on
page 202. Makes 4 servings.

RUSH HOUR TIP

Easy Pasta Toss also makes a nice, quick dinner. To add
more "substance" and protein, toss in some cooked and
shredded chicken. This also makes a great side dish!

*Make pasta more fun by coloring it! Either use
colored pasta from your local market or add a
touch of food coloring to your water.*

"PITA SOUP"

No, don't fret—there aren't any pitas in this soup, but pita sandwiches and this soup make a perfect light and healthy meal.

4 cans chicken broth
2 cups cooked chicken, cubed or
   torn
1 cup frozen peas
½ teaspoon salt
¼ teaspoon pepper
1 cup noodles of choice
1 cup sliced carrots
1 cup chopped celery stalks
1-2 cups cooked instant rice (optional)

Heat all ingredients, excluding noodles in a saucepan. Bring to boiling. Add noodles then reduce heat and simmer 10-15 minutes or until vegetables and noodles are tender. Add 1-2 cups cooked rice at the end of cooking, if desired. Serve with Pita Calzone Sandwich recipe on following page. Makes 6 servings.

PITA CALZONE SANDWICHES

6 pita pockets
2 cups cubed cooked chicken
1 cup broccoli florets
1 cup shredded reduced-fat Cheddar cheese

Preheat oven to 250 degrees. Mix broccoli, chicken and cheese in small bowl. Fill pita pockets with mixture and bake for 10 minutes or until cheese is melted. Baking these pitas give them a calzone-like quality. Makes 6 servings.

RUSH HOUR TIP:

Pita bread is one of those foods that begs us to be experimental. It's a great "make your own" dish to serve to kids with a variety of filling choices. Try the following combinations and while you're being creative, why not make up some of your own?

TACO PITA – Mix leftover taco fixings together and toss in a pita. Warm in oven then add lettuce and tomato.

HAM & CHEESE – Try cubed ham, shredded cheese. Bake for 10 minutes in a 250-degree oven or until cheese is melted and bubbly.

VEGGIE PITA – Sliced tomato, avocado, 'sprouts, crisp cucumber topped with low-fat ranch dressing

B.L.T. PITA – Bacon, lettuce and tomato tucked in a pita

FAMOUS FIESTA CASSEROLE

1 pound ground beef
1 can condensed tomato soup
1 soup can of water
3 teaspoons chili powder
1 teaspoon onion powder
2 cups shredded Cheddar cheese
1 cup sour cream
½ bunch diced green onions
1½ cups chopped tomato
4 cups broken tortilla chips

Preheat oven to 350 degrees. Brown beef in a skillet over medium heat. Add soup and can of water. Stir in chili powder and onion powder. Let simmer for 10-20 minutes. Place broken chips on the bottom of a casserole dish. Top with beef mixture. Top beef mixture with sour cream, onions, chopped tomato and cheese. Bake for 20 minutes. Serve with Simple Salad (below) and French bread. Makes 6 servings.

SIMPLE SALAD

1 small head of lettuce, washed, dried and torn into bite-sized
   pieces
1 small red onion, peeled and sliced thinly
12 cherry tomatoes, quartered
½ cup shredded carrot
½ cup dressing (your choice of store-bought or pick a
   Dazzling Dressing Recipe from pages 29-32).

Toss all ingredients together, except dressing. Add dressing just prior to serving. Makes 4 large salads or 8 side salads.

For a more kid-friendly salad, serve lettuce tomatoes, onions and carrots as optional ingredients.

Week One Grocery List

Produce

- 1½ cup carrots
- ½ bunch green onions
- 1 cup broccoli florets
- 3 tomatoes
- Fresh parsley
- Garlic-cloves or minced garlic
- 5 large baking potatoes
- 1 cup celery stalks
- Lemon juice
- 1 head lettuce*
- 1 red onion*
- 12 cherry tomatoes*
- Fruit (for fruit salad to be served with Ham and Swiss Pizza)

Breads

- 1 (12-inch) Italian bread shell
- 6 pita pockets
- 1 loaf French bread

Canned/Boxed goods

- 4 cans chicken broth
- 1 can tomato soup
- 1 bag tortilla chips
- Dijon-style mustard
- 16 ounces linguine
- 1 cup noodles of choice
- 2 cups instant rice, optional

Pantry

- Salt
- Chili powder
- Pepper
- Onion powder
- Flour
- Bread crumbs
- Dried parsley

Meat

- 4 cups cubed cooked chicken
- 6 boneless skinless chicken breasts
- 6 ounces ham, diced
- 1 pound ground beef

Dairy

- 1¼ cups Swiss cheese
- 3 cups Cheddar cheese
- 1½ cups sour cream
- 1½ sticks butter
- ½ cup milk

Frozen

- 1 cup frozen peas

Other

- Dressing* for Simple Salad (or add ingredients from pages 29-32 for a homemade dressing)
- Toppings of choice for Choose-A-Way Breadsticks (see page 202).

- _____
- _____
- _____
- _____
- _____
- _____

NOTES:

Week Two Menu

COVERED CHICKEN
SIMPLE SALAD

•

CHICKEN AND POTATOES SKILLET
ROSEMARY BROCCOLI

•

ALMOST ORIENTAL NOODLE DISH

•

CHICKEN STROGANOFF
SIMPLE SALAD

•

FRENCH BREAD PIZZAS

COVERED CHICKEN

2 pounds potatoes, cut into ¼-inch slices
2 onions, sliced thinly
2 tablespoons butter
3 slices bacon, chopped
1 pound boneless, skinless chicken breasts, chopped
2½ cups chicken stock
Salt and pepper to taste

Preheat oven to 300 degrees. Layer ½ of the potato slices in a spray-coated, 2-quart casserole. Cover potatoes with ½ the onion. Heat the butter in a skillet and brown chicken and bacon. Drain and add to the casserole. Top chicken with remaining onion and another layer of potatoes. Pour chicken stock over casserole. Cover tightly and bake for 2 hours or until chicken is done and potatoes are tender. Serve with a Simple Salad (page 64). Makes 6 servings.

CHICKEN AND POTATOES SKILLET

6 boneless, skinless chicken breasts
1½ cup water
2 envelopes chicken gravy mix
Your choice of the following:
1 (4.5 ounce) can of sliced mushrooms
2 potatoes, peeled and cubed
1 cup baby carrots, halved
1 cup broccoli florets
1 can niblets corn
Salt and pepper to taste

Cook chicken over medium heat for 10-15 minutes or until no longer pink. Remove from pan. Mix water and gravy-mix in bowl and then add to skillet. Add any "extras." Heat to boiling and then simmer for five minutes or until tender. Return chicken to pan, cover and heat for a few minutes until heated through. Serve with Rosemary Broccoli (page 134). Makes 6 servings.

ALMOST ORIENTAL NOODLE DISH

1 pound beef boneless sirloin, cut into strips
1 can (14.5 ounce) beef broth
¼ cup teriyaki sauce
2 cups rice noodles
1½ cups pea pods, if desired

Cook beef in a skillet over medium-high heat for 4 minutes or until brown; set aside. In same skillet mix broth, teriyaki sauce and pea pods. Add noodles. Cook over medium heat for three minutes or until noodles are tender. Return beef to skillet and cook for an additional 2-3 minutes or until sauce thickens slightly. Makes 4 servings.

The small amount of teriyaki sauce used in this recipe gives it a nice flavor without being too strong for most kids' tastes. If teriyaki sauce is a problem, serve kids sirloin with plain noodles on the side.

THE RAW RULE

Try to serve a raw fruit or vegetable with every meal. I guarantee you will pack in a load of extra vitamins if you add this rule to your repertoire.

AWESOME APPETIZERS

One of the best ways to naturally reduce how much food you eat at each meal is to have a nice salad 20 minutes prior to the main course. Salad is quite filling! A glass of water is another way to naturally reduce hunger. Try a salad and a glass of water prior to your meals. I know you'll see the difference. This is a great habit for kids to learn! If your kids aren't salad-eaters, try a glass of water with fresh vegetables, like carrots, broccoli, celery, etc. with ranch dressing. By prioritizing our vegetables before our meals, we don't run the risk of becoming so full of the "main course" we forget to leave room for the all important side dish.

CHICKEN STROGANOFF

4 boneless, skinless chicken breasts
2 tablespoons olive oil
1 onion, sliced thinly
8 ounces mushrooms, sliced
1¼ cups nonfat sour cream
Salt and pepper to taste
16 ounces egg noodles

Prepare noodles according to package directions. Place chicken breasts between waxed paper and pound to ¼-inch thickness. Cut each breast into 1-inch strips. Set aside. Heat oil in a nonstick skillet coated with cooking spray, add onion and cook till transparent. Add the mushrooms and cook until golden brown. Set mushroom mixture aside; cover to keep warm. Add the other tablespoon of oil to skillet and fry the chicken strips 5-8 minutes, or until lightly browned and no longer pink inside. Add mushroom and onion mixture back to the pan. Stir in sour cream and bring to a boil. Heat through and serve immediately. Serve with Simple Salad (page 64). Makes 4 servings.

FRENCH BREAD PIZZAS

1 loaf French bread
3 cups cheese, your choice, shredded
1 jar pizza sauce
1 pound of meat, your choice:
  ground round, Italian sausage,
  pepperoni or bacon pieces (or go
  vegetarian and use freshly chopped
  vegetables of choice)

Preheat oven to 400 degrees. Cook meat over medium heat until done. Add pizza sauce and stir. Cut French bread into 6 equal size slices. Pour meat mixture over French bread, spreading evenly. Top with cheese and bake for 10-15 minutes or until cheese is melted and bread is toasted. Makes 6 servings.

Week Two Grocery List

Produce
- [ ] 2 pounds +3 potatoes
- [ ] 1 cup baby carrots
- [ ] 1 cup broccoli florets
- [ ] 1½ cups pea pods (if desired)
- [ ] 2 onions
- [ ] 2 heads lettuce*
- [ ] 24 cherry tomatoes*
- [ ] 1 cup shredded carrot*
- [ ] 2 small red onions*
- [ ] 2 pounds broccoli**

Breads
- [ ] 1 loaf French bread

Canned/Boxed Goods
- [ ] 4.5 ounce can of mushrooms
- [ ] 1 can niblets corn
- [ ] 2 envelopes chicken gravy mix
- [ ] 2½ cups chicken broth/or stock
- [ ] 1 can beef broth
- [ ] ¼ cup teriyaki sauce
- [ ] 2 cups rice noodles
- [ ] 1 jar pizza sauce
- [ ] 16 ounces egg noodles

Meat
- [ ] 1 pound ground round, Italian sausage, pepperoni or bacon pieces—your choice
- [ ] 1 pound beef boneless sirloin
- [ ] 6 boneless, skinless chicken breasts
- [ ] 3 sliced bacon
- [ ] 1 pound boneless, skinless chicken breasts, chopped

Dairy
- [ ] 3 cups shredded cheese-mozzarella or mixture
- [ ] Butter
- [ ] 1¼ cup nonfat sour cream

Pantry
- [ ] Olive oil
- [ ] Salt
- [ ] Pepper
- [ ] Rosemary**

Other
- [ ] Dressing* of choice for 2 Simple Salads (or add ingredients from one of the recipes on pages 29-32.)
- [ ] Lemon juice**
- [ ] _____
- [ ] _____
- [ ] _____
- [ ] _____
- [ ] _____
- [ ] _____
- [ ] _____
- [ ] _____
- [ ] _____
- [ ] _____
- [ ] _____
- [ ] _____
- [ ] _____
- [ ] _____
- [ ] _____
- [ ] _____

*These ingredients are for the Simple Salad (pg. 64) to be served with the Covered Chicken and the Chicken Stroganoff (p. 70)

**These ingredients are for the Rosemary Broccoli (pg. 134) to be served with the Chicken and Potatoes Skillet.

NOTES:

_____

_____

_____

_____

_____

_____

_____

_____

_____

_____

_____

_____

_____

_____

_____

_____

_____

Week Three Menu

TACO NACHO SALAD

○

KID-FRIENDLY SLOPPY JOES
PRETTY PASTA SALAD

○

MAKE-MINE-A-MELT
POTATO WEDGES

○

SCRUMPTIOUS SWISS STRATA

○

CHICKEN IN WHINE SAUCE
POUPON POTATOES

TACO-NACHO SALAD

I call this Taco-Nacho Salad because I often find myself fixing it two ways. My daughter loves nachos whereas my husband and I prefer taco salads. This recipe makes it easy to create both in a snap.

1 onion, chopped
1 green bell pepper, chopped
1 cup prepared salsa
½ cup frozen corn, thawed and cooked
6 cups torn lettuce leaves
Corn tortilla chips
1 cup shredded cheese, Cheddar or taco cheese
½ pound ground round
Low-fat or nonfat sour cream (optional)

TO MAKE NACHOS:

Spread chips on a plate and heat in 200-degree oven for 5 minutes. Brown beef over medium heat until cooked. Mix in salsa and heat thoroughly. Spread meat mixture over warmed chips. Top with bell pepper, corn, onion and shredded cheese. Dip in sour cream if desired. Makes 6 servings.

For super kid-friendly fare, omit the onion, pepper and corn. Chips topped with meat and melted cheese are sure to be a hit!

TO MAKE SALAD:

Crush chips and place in a shallow bowl. Top with lettuce, then proceed with meat mixture and remaining toppings as listed above. Makes 4 large salads, 6 side salads.

RUSH HOUR TIP:

Turn up the heat: If you think more spice is nice use a shredded pepper cheese and a high-temp salsa.

KID-FRIENDLY SLOPPY JOES

1 cup barbecue sauce
½ cup ketchup
8 hamburger buns

1 cup water
2 pounds ground round

Combine all ingredients (excluding buns) in a saucepan over medium heat. Cook on low for 10-15 minutes and then scoop onto buns and serve. Serve with Pretty Pasta Salad (below). Makes 8 servings.

PRETTY PASTA SALAD

2 cups cooked rotini
½ cup mayonnaise
1 tablespoon vinegar

2 cups cherry-tomatoes, halved
¼ cup Parmesan cheese
½ teaspoon salt

Mix all ingredients together in a medium serving bowl. Cover with plastic wrap and refrigerate for two hours before serving. Makes 4 servings.

This dish can be made completely kid friendly by holding out the cherry-tomatoes and scooping the child's portion into a separate bowl before adding them to the mix.

RUSH HOUR TIP:

Pasta salad makes a great snack. Scoop some into small plastic storage containers and leave in the fridge for a quick bite. Keeps 3-4 days. To make a satisfying lunch add a baguette or nice piece of bread.

MAKE MINE A MELT

1-2 bagel halves per person
Bagel bar of toppings:
>Slices of cheese, Swiss, mozzarella, Cheddar, etc.
>Meat of choice, diced chicken, cubed ham, etc.
>Vegetables like green onions, mushrooms, onions, broccoli florets

Do this dinner assembly-line style. Let each person choose one or two bagel halves and top with their choice of goodies. Broil until cheese is melted and bagels are slightly toasted. Serve with Potato Wedges (below).

POTATO WEDGES

4 potatoes, cut into 6 wedges each
Cooking spray or butter spray
Salt
Paprika for color (optional)
Ketchup or ranch dressing for serving

Preheat oven to 400 degrees. Line potatoes on a cookie sheet sprayed with nonstick cooking spray. Sprinkle potatoes with salt. Add paprika if you wish. Bake for 20-30 minutes or until tender. Don't forget to put ketchup on the table! Makes 8 servings
(3 wedges each).

SCRUMPTIOUS SWISS STRATA*

Often thought of as a breakfast dish, strata is so filling it also makes a great dinner choice.

6 cups French bread, cubed   2 cups milk
2 cups shredded Swiss cheese   4 eggs, beaten
1½ cups cubed ham

Place ½ of the French bread cubes in a casserole dish. Top with 1 cup of cheese and the ham. Layer on remaining bread cubes. In a bowl, whisk together eggs and milk. Pour over the layered casserole, saturating thoroughly. Top with remaining cheese. Cover and refrigerate for 3 hours minimum, but preferably overnight. To cook, bake in a 325-degree oven for 40 minutes or until knife inserted in center comes out clean. Let stand 5-10 minutes before serving.

*This is an easy dish for a make-ahead menu. Assemble the strata the night before and refrigerate. Complete cooking the next day and enjoy. Makes 6 servings.

Kids not crazy about Swiss cheese? Try Cheddar cheese instead.

CHICKEN IN WHINE SAUCE

No that isn't a typo, but for a kid-friendly benefit I was trying to hide the wine! (To make this kid friendly simply take out the kids' chicken, slice into strips, bread and bake—see Children's Chicken Tenders p. 82. Serve with an array of dipping sauces... i.e. ranch dressing, B.B.Q. sauce, ketchup). As author Leanne Ely shared with us in *Healthy Foods*—you name it; if kids can dip it, they'll likely eat it.

6 boneless, skinless chicken breasts   ¼ cup flour
3 cups sliced mushrooms   ½ cup dry white wine
½ cup Dijon-style mustard   Vegetable oil

To continue with the adult recipe, coat chicken with flour and then brown in hot vegetable oil. Remove from pan. Stir mushrooms into pan drippings and heat for several minutes. Add mustard and wine, then return chicken to pan. Heat to boiling, then reduce heat. Cover and simmer 25 minutes or until chicken is no longer pink. Serve with Poupon Potatoes (below). Makes 6 servings.

POUPON POTATOES

1 pound cubed potatoes   1 small onion, chopped
⅓ cup Dijon-style mustard   ¼ cup olive oil

Mix mustard and oil together. Add potatoes and onions and toss. Spread in a baking pan and cook for 45 to 50 minutes in a 400-degree oven. Makes 4 side servings.

Week Three Grocery List:

Produce
- ❑ 3 cups mushrooms
- ❑ 4 baking potatoes
- ❑ 1 pound potatoes, cubed
- ❑ 3-4 onions
- ❑ 1 head lettuce
- ❑ 1 green bell pepper
- ❑ 2 cups cherry-tomatoes
- ❑ Assorted vegetables for melts (green onions, mushrooms, broccoli)

Breads
- ❑ 6 cups French bread
- ❑ Bagels, 1 per person
- ❑ 8 hamburger buns

Canned/Boxed Goods
- ❑ Rotini pasta
- ❑ Salsa
- ❑ Dijon-style mustard
- ❑ Ketchup
- ❑ Barbecue sauce
- ❑ Mayonnaise
- ❑ Corn tortilla chips
- ❑ Ranch dressing

Pantry/Spices
- ❑ Flour
- ❑ Vegetable oil
- ❑ Vinegar
- ❑ Salt
- ❑ Olive oil

- ❑ Cooking spray
- ❑ Paprika

Meat
- ❑ 2½ pounds ground round
- ❑ 1½ cups ham
- ❑ 6 boneless, skinless chicken breasts
- ❑ Meat for melts (diced chicken, cubed ham, etc.)

Dairy
- ❑ 2 cups milk
- ❑ Parmesan cheese
- ❑ 2 cups shredded Swiss cheese
- ❑ Slices of cheese for melts
- ❑ 4 eggs
- ❑ Sour cream
- ❑ 1 cup shredded Cheddar or taco cheese

Frozen
- ❑ ½ cup frozen corn

Other
- ❑ ½ cup dry white wine
- ❑ _____
- ❑ _____
- ❑ _____
- ❑ _____
- ❑ _____
- ❑ _____
- ❑ _____

NOTES:

Week Four Menu

CHICKEN TENDERS
POTATO WEDGES

○

PARMESAN ROTINI
QUESADILLA BITES

○

PRESTO PRIMAVERA
CORN ON THE COB

○

PERFECT PORK CHOPS
DIJON POTATOES

○

2+2+2+2 = TURKEY
STORE-BOUGHT STUFFING
GLORIOUS GREEN BEANS

CHILDREN'S CHICKEN TENDERS

1 egg
⅛ cup butter, melted
⅛ cup grated Parmesan cheese
1 cup crushed butter crackers
1 pound chicken tenders
Paprika to taste
Salt and pepper to taste

Preheat oven to 375 degrees. Beat egg with a fork. Place melted butter in separate bowl. Mix crackers and spices in a third bowl. Dip tenders into egg, then cracker mixture, then butter. Sprinkle with Parmesan cheese. Bake for 15-20 minutes or until chicken is no longer pink. Serve with Potato Wedges (page 76). Makes 4 servings.

RUSH HOUR TIP:

Adult Adaptation: If you are not a chicken-tender eater, Tear up some romaine lettuce, cut tenders into bite-sized pieces and toss in salad. Top with one of the Dazzling Dressings from pages 29-32).

PARMESAN ROTINI

3 cups rotini pasta, uncooked
10 ounces frozen chopped broccoli
6 ounces pre-cooked chicken breast
   strips
2 tablespoons olive oil
½ cup grated Parmesan cheese
1 tomato, cut into bite-sized pieces

Cook rotini according to package directions, drain. Steam broccoli. Combine cheese, broccoli, chicken, Parmesan and tomato with pasta. Toss to mix. Cook on low setting until warmed through. Serve with Quesadilla Bites (page 84). Makes 10 servings.

CORN ON THE COB

Corn on the cob is a vegetable that kids usually love and is easy to make.

6 cobs of corn, shucked
Butter
Water

Fill a large covered saucepan with 2 inches of water and bring to a boil. Place corn in boiling water, cover and return to boiling. Reduce heat to low and simmer 8-10 minutes, or until tender. Avoid overcooking. Serve with Presto Primavera (below). Makes 6 servings.

PRESTO PRIMAVERA

8 ounces penne pasta
8 ounces frozen peas
8 ounces frozen green
   beans
2 large carrots, sliced
2 tomatoes, chopped
Salt and pepper to taste
Parmesan cheese

Cook pasta according to
package directions; drain. Meanwhile, heat peas, green beans, carrots and tomatoes in separate large saucepan. When pasta is done, add to vegetable mixture and heat through. Season with salt and pepper, if desired. Top with Parmesan cheese. Makes 4-6 servings.

QUESADILLA BITES

1½ cups mozzarella cheese
1 cup chicken, cooked and shredded
8 flour tortillas
½ teaspoon cayenne pepper

Sprinkle mozzarella cheese and chicken over tortillas. Cut tortillas into quarters and fold over. Cook in a skillet over medium heat until insides are melted. (You can also microwave these for 20 seconds or until cheese has just melted.) Makes 8 servings.

Tortillas make great snacks! Whole-wheat tortillas are a healthier choice and can be found at most supermarkets. Simply place favorite toppings on tortillas, microwave for 20 seconds and voila!

THE ELECTRONIC SUPERMARKET

Too busy to shop? Look no further, the Internet has come to the rescue of busy cooks once again. Virtual Supermarkets are popping up left and right. With a few clicks of a button, you can order your groceries online, save frequently used shopping lists, and watch for delivery at your door. Consider entering the grocery lists from this book for those crazy, busy weeks when traveling to the store isn't an option. The charges for electronic grocery shopping vary, but many sites offer very reasonable rates that are well worth the time you will save—not to mention the nutrition you will gain over other quick fix solutions—like pizza!

Here are a few popular stores you may want to investigate:
www.netgrocer.com   www.shopthepig.com
www.deandeluca.com   www.peapod.com
www.safeway.com   www.traderjoes.com

PERFECT PORK CHOPS

6 bone-in pork chops
½ cup Dijon-style mustard
1 cup crushed corn flakes
Salt and pepper to taste

Preheat oven to 350 degrees. Spread mustard over chops and then dredge in corn flakes. Place on a baking sheet in a single layer and salt and pepper to taste. Bake for 30 minutes or until no longer pink. Serve with Dijon Potatoes (below). Makes 6 servings.

DIJON POTATOES

4 medium potatoes, sliced   ½ cup Dijon-style mustard
3 tablespoons flour   2 tablespoons butter
1½ cups milk   ½ cup shredded Swiss cheese

Preheat oven to 350 degrees. Mix flour and milk and heat in saucepan over medium heat. Cook until mixture thickens. Add mustard, stir and heat through. In a greased casserole dish, layer potatoes and milk mixture. Top with cheese. Bake for 15 minutes or until cheese is melted and potatoes are warmed through. Makes 4 servings.

2+2+2+2 = TURKEY

2 pounds boneless, skinless turkey breast, cubed
2 cups Italian dressing
2 cups chicken broth
2 packages mixed frozen vegetables
Store-bought stuffing for serving

Brown cubed turkey over medium heat. Mix turkey and remaining ingredients in Dutch oven. Bring to boiling and then simmer for 15 minutes, or until turkey is fully cooked. Serve with store-bought stuffing such as Stove-Top® and Glorious Green Beans (below). Makes 8 servings.

GLORIOUS GREEN BEANS

1 pound fresh green beans, washed and ends trimmed
⅛ cup slivered almonds
⅛ cup red wine vinegar
Water

Fill a saucepan with 2 inches water and bring to a boil. Cut green beans into 2-inch pieces and place in a steamer or colander in saucepan. Steam for 5-6 minutes or until crisp-tender. Transfer beans to serving bowl. Add vinegar and almonds; toss. Makes 4 servings.

GREEN BEAN BASICS

Serving Size: Allow ¼ cup of beans per serving.
Storage: Store green beans in a plastic bag in your refrigerator. Beans last about 5 days when stored this way.
Preparation: Always rinse and drain beans. If there are strings, remove them. Snap off the ends of the beans before cooking.

Week Four Grocery List

Produce
- [ ] 3 tomatoes
- [ ] 4 medium baking potatoes
- [ ] 6 cobs of corn
- [ ] 1 pound fresh green beans
- [ ] 2 large carrots

Canned/Boxed Goods
- [ ] Butter crackers
- [ ] Rotini pasta
- [ ] Penne pasta
- [ ] Corn flakes
- [ ] 2 cups Italian dressing
- [ ] 2 cups chicken broth
- [ ] Dijon-style mustard
- [ ] Red wine vinegar
- [ ] 1 package store-bought stuffing (such as Stove-Top®)

Pantry/Spices
- [ ] Paprika
- [ ] Salt
- [ ] Pepper
- [ ] Olive oil
- [ ] Cayenne pepper
- [ ] Flour
- [ ] ⅛ cup slivered almonds

Meat
- [ ] 2 pounds boneless, skinless turkey breast
- [ ] 6 bone-in pork chops
- [ ] 6 ounces chicken, pre-cooked for strips
- [ ] 1 cup cooked and shredded chicken
- [ ] 1 pound chicken tenders

Dairy
- [ ] 1 egg
- [ ] Parmesan cheese
- [ ] 1 stick butter
- [ ] ½ cup Swiss cheese
- [ ] 1½ cups mozzarella cheese
- [ ] 1½ cups milk
- [ ] 8 flour tortillas (most are located in the dairy section by the cheese)

Frozen
- [ ] 10 ounces frozen chopped broccoli
- [ ] 2 packages frozen vegetable mix
- [ ] ½ pound frozen green beans
- [ ] ½ pound frozen peas

Other
- [ ] _____
- [ ] _____
- [ ] _____
- [ ] _____
- [ ] _____
- [ ] _____
- [ ] _____
- [ ] _____

NOTES:

CLASSIC CHICKEN BAKE
SUGAR CARROTS

o

PRESTO MAC
VERY GARLIC-Y CAESAR SALAD

o

CHRISTMAS EVE CHILI

o

SAMMY'S FAVORITE NOODLE BAKE

o

LET-ME-SOAK CHICKEN
CHEESY SCALLOPED SPUDS

CLASSIC CHICKEN BAKE

1 pound chicken, cut into bite-sized pieces
1½ cups water
1 can (10-3/4 ounce) condensed cream of chicken soup
2 cups instant white rice, uncooked

Preheat oven to 350 degrees. Mix soup and water over medium heat until well-blended. Transfer to baking dish. Stir in chicken and rice. Cover and bake for 20 minutes, or until chicken is no longer pink and casserole is heated through and bubbly. Serve with Sugar Carrots (below). Makes 6 servings.

SUGAR CARROTS

My Mom made these carrots as our "vegetable" one night. Not liking cooked carrots to begin with, I wasn't too excited by her choice. All that changed when I had my first bite. My daughter and I agreed that if this counted as a vegetable, you could count us in!

1 large package fresh carrots
3-4 tablespoons butter, or to taste
2-3 tablespoons brown sugar, or to taste

Cut fresh, peeled carrots into julienne strips. Simmer in pan of water till fork tender. Drain. Melt in the butter and brown sugar to coat the carrots until well-glazed. Makes 6 servings.

In our house we practice the "one-bite" rule. Our daughter isn't forced to eat an entire meal she loathes, although she is required to try one bite of each new food. A friend suggested this to us and we were pleased to discover this added many new foods to her "edible repertoire".

PRESTO MAC

1 pound dried elbow macaroni
2 cups shredded Cheddar cheese
3 large eggs
¼ teaspoon pepper

⅓ cup butter
½ cup bread crumbs
2 cups milk
¼ teaspoon salt

Preheat oven to400 degrees. Cook macaroni just until tender. Drain. Return macaroni to pan. Remove from heat. Add butter and ¾ cup cheese and stir. Spray a casserole dish with cooking spray. Sprinkle some cheese and ½ of the bread crumbs on the bottom of the casserole dish. In a bowl, combine eggs, milk, salt and pepper. Add this mixture to macaroni and stir well. Transfer mixture to casserole dish. Top with remaining cheese and remaining bread crumbs. Bake for 15-20 minutes, until warm and bubbly. Serve with Very Garlic-y Caesar Salad (page 92). Makes 6-8 servings.

PASTA HINTS & TIPS

*For soups, always choose tiny pasta so it "scoops" easily with a spoon. Orzo and farfelle are two good examples. Likewise for casseroles that contain pasta, stick with smaller noodles like penne or elbow macaroni. If making a layered casserole, try lasagna or another wide flat noodle.

*To avoid sticky-pasta masses, add 2 tablespoons of oil per gallon of water.

*For even cooking, make sure that the pasta is completely immersed in the water.

*Stir pasta immediately after immersing in water to help eliminate clumping.

*If you will be using the pasta in a casserole, slightly undercook on the stove. It will complete its cooking process during baking.

*To reheat pasta, drop it into boiling water and let stand for 2 minutes. Drain and serve.

VERY GARLIC-Y CHICKEN CAESAR SALAD

12 ounces skinless chicken breast, grilled (or use leftovers)
1 head romaine lettuce, chopped
½ cup croutons (make your own)
2 cloves garlic, pressed
2 teaspoons lemon juice
½ teaspoon Dijon-style mustard
⅛ cup Romano cheese
2 tablespoons red wine vinegar
¼ cup olive oil
1 teaspoon Worcestershire sauce
Salt and pepper to taste
2 ounces anchovies fillets, mashed (optional)

Make croutons first by chopping up stale bread, brushing with olive oil and sprinkling with a little garlic powder. Toast in 350-degree oven till brown—probably no more than 10 minutes. Check them often, though! Wash romaine and chop into bite-sized pieces. Normally, you only want to tear lettuce, but if you are going to be using it right away, chop away and save yourself some time. In a bowl, combine oil, vinegar, Worcestershire, salt and pepper to taste, garlic, lemon juice, anchovies and mustard. Or use a blender. Just prior to serving, toss lettuce and dressing, half the cheese and croutons in large bowl. Serve on individual plates and top with chicken and remaining cheese. Makes 4 servings.

Very Garlic-y Chicken Caesar Salad excerpted from Healthy Foods, an irreverent guide to understanding nutrition and feeding your family well by Leanne Ely, C.N.C. ISBN:1891400207

RUSH HOUR TIP

When tossing salads, always add dressing at the last possible minute. This will prevent salads from getting soggy or wilted.

CHRISTMAS-EVE CHILI

Always a bit rebellious, we started a tradition of making Chili on Christmas Eve when we realized that the thought of making a large meal with tons of dishes didn't seem appealing the day before the big event! We've tried many recipes over the years, all fighting for the title of "Christmas Chili Champion." Below you'll find our favorite as of 2003...

Chili is by far one of the freezer-friendliest dishes! Consider doubling or tripling this recipe and storing some away in freezer containers. To reheat, transfer container to refrigerator and let thaw overnight. Warm over medium heat until heated through. Make sure to let the chili cool prior to freezing, this helps avoid ice crystals. Also, leave at least an inch of headroom in the container when filling.

1 pound lean ground beef
1 (14.5 ounce) can
   Mexican-style stewed
   Tomatoes

1 small can tomato paste
½ teaspoon cumin
¼ teaspoon salt

Choose as many as you like:

1 medium onion, chopped
2 cloves garlic, minced
1 can corn
1 (14.5 ounce) can kidney
   beans
1 tablespoon red pepper
   flakes
⅛ cup jarred jalapenos
   (include the juice if you
   like really hot chili)

2 jalapeno peppers, diced
   into thin slices
1 red bell pepper, chopped
1 green pepper, chopped
3 tablespoons chili powder
1 tablespoon oregano
1 tablespoon basil leaves
1 tablespoon Cajun spice
   mix

Choose one or a combo of 2:

1 cup red wine
1 bottle of beer

1 cup of coffee
1 cup beef broth

Choose one "secret" ingredient...

1 tablespoon brown sugar
1 tablespoon sugar
3 Hershey Kisses® or 2 tablespoons chocolate chips

1 tablespoon cocoa
1 teaspoon instant coffee
¼ teaspoon cinnamon

Choose one (or none)

Instant white rice
Elbow macaroni (or whatever pasta is in the pantry)

Brown meat in a large skillet over medium heat until brown. Drain. If you have chosen bell peppers, garlic or onion, add them to the meat and cook another minute or two. Add all other ingredients you have chosen, stirring well. Cook on medium heat for 5-10 minutes and then reduce heat to low for at least 40 minutes. Of course, as with most soups, stews and chili recipes—the longer they cook, the more the flavors meld. For great tasting flavor, try putting this recipe together in the morning and then leaving it in a slow cooker on low setting for a great dinner meal. If desired, prepare rice or macaroni in a separate pan. Place pasta or rice in bottom of bowl and top with chili. Makes 4-6 servings.

THE RUSH HOUR COOK RECOMMENDS...

Although I don't like jalapenos, there is one time I will use them in cooking and that is in chili. I usually make chili in 2 pound batches and I will use 3-4 jalapeno peppers. I seed and slice them into small circles and add them during the simmering process. Wow. They give a hot and somewhat sweet taste to chili that is out of this world. We always serve our chili over rice or elbow macaroni so that helps "tone down the heat" for those who don't like it quite so hot. I also make a triple "base" of the chili and then separate it into thee large pots so I can have a Super-Spicy version, Medium-Spiced version and Kids' version.

SAMANTHA'S FAVORITE NOODLE BAKE

Before I became the Rush Hour Cook, there were two recipes that my family would actually request—(the rest of the time they banned me from the kitchen.) Below, you'll find one of them.

1 package of penne pasta
1 container fat-free ricotta cheese
1 bag of part-skim mozzarella cheese
1 pound lean ground beef
3 garlic cloves, minced
1 jar prepared spaghetti sauce (like Ragu™)
1 cup chopped onion
1 cup sliced mushrooms

Preheat oven to 350 degrees. Cook and drain pasta according to directions. While pasta is cooking, brown beef over medium heat in a non-stick skillet. Drain.

If kids will be dining with you this evening, this is your last chance to reserve some browned beef to keep separate from the forthcoming onion, mushrooms and garlic. I usually reserve ½ cup for my daughter, and then mix and bake hers separately. If your child is a spaghetti lover, consider making this recipe for the adults and reserving some noodles and plain sauce for a child's spaghetti plate.

Add mushrooms, onion and garlic. Return to heat and cook for 2-3 more minutes or until onion is transparent. Add the jar of spaghetti sauce and simmer over low heat for 10 minutes. While this is simmering, combine ricotta cheese and ⅔ of the mozzarella cheese in a bowl.

Spray a baking dish with cooking spray and then layer your ingredients, beginning with a pasta layer on the bottom. Cover with meat, then cheese. Bake for 30 minutes. Top with remaining mozzarella cheese and bake for another 5 minutes

or until melted.   Serve with a warm loaf of French bread.
Makes 12 servings.

:::
This is a great recipe for freezing. I usually divide the bake
into two dishes. I cook one and then package the other for
the freezer. You can also purchase individual-serving-size
aluminum tins at your local grocer. Use these tins to make
individual bake-servings that can be eaten for lunch or on
nights when people are "eating on the run".
:::

LET-ME-SOAK CHICKEN

This is especially delicious when prepared on a grill!

Olive oil or fat-free Italian dressing (½ bottle, or enough to
  cover chicken)
1 chicken breast for each person
Fresh rosemary
1 lemon, cut into wedges
Salt and pepper to taste

Place chicken breasts in a shallow
glass pan. Add enough oil or
dressing to cover. Add sprigs of
rosemary to oil. Squeeze lemon
over chicken then drop the wedges
into marinade mixture. Let sit for
at least an hour—though the
longer the better. (In my ideal
world, I remember to do this in the
morning and then we grill at
night.) Makes 6 servings.

To cook, grill for a delicious flavor—five minutes on each side
or until done. Or toss in a frying pan and do the same, or bake
for 30 minutes. Serve with Cheesy Scalloped Spuds (page 97).

CHEESY SCALLOPED SPUDS

6 potatoes, peeled and sliced
3 tablespoons butter, melted
½ teaspoon salt
¼ teaspoon pepper
1 cup shredded Swiss or Cheddar cheese, divided
1 cup milk

Preheat oven to 425 degrees. Arrange ½ of the potato slices in an 11 x 7-inch casserole dish coated with cooking spray. Drizzle 2 tablespoons of melted butter over potatoes. Add ½ of the salt, pepper and ⅓ cup cheese. Repeat layers. Drizzle with remaining tablespoon of butter. Bring milk to a low boil in a small saucepan and pour over the layered mixture. Top with final ⅓ cup cheese Bake for 40-50 minutes or until potatoes are tender.

Week Five Grocery List

Produce

- 1 large package fresh carrots
- 1 head romaine lettuce
- 1 head garlic
- 1 lemon
- 3 onions
- 6 potatoes
- Optional for chili (jalapenos, red bell pepper, green bell pepper)
- Fresh rosemary

Canned/Boxed Goods

- 2 cups white instant rice
- 1 can condensed cream of chicken soup
- 1 pound dried elbow macaroni
- Croutons
- 1 can tomato paste
- 1 can Mexican-style stewed tomatoes
- 1 can corn (optional for chili)
- 1 can kidney beans (optional for chili)
- 1 can beef broth (optional for chili)
- 1 package penne pasta
- Fat-free Italian dressing for marinating (or olive oil)
- 1 jar prepared spaghetti sauce (Ragu, etc)
- Dijon-style mustard
- Worcestershire sauce
- Lemon juice

- Anchovies (for Caesar salad)
- ⅛ cup jarred jalapenos

Pantry/Spices

- Brown sugar
- Pepper
- Bread crumbs
- Salt
- Red wine vinegar
- Olive oil
- Sugar
- Cumin
- Optional spices (chili powder, oregano, basil, red pepper flakes, Cajun spice mix, chocolate chips, cocoa, Hershey Kisses™, cinnamon)

Meat

- 2 pounds lean ground beef
- 1 chicken breast per person for Let-Me-Soak-Chicken
- 1 pound chicken, for bite sized pieces
- 12 ounces chicken breasts, without skin, grilled for Caesar salad

Dairy

- 2 sticks butter
- 1 cup milk
- 3 eggs
- 2 cups shredded Cheddar cheese

- ☐ 1 cup Swiss or cheddar cheese for potatoes
- ☐ 1 container fat-free ricotta cheese
- ☐ 1 bag of part-skim mozzarella cheese
- ☐ ⅛ cup Romano cheese

Miscellaneous (optional for chili)

- ☐ 1 cup red wine
- ☐ 1 bottle of beer

- ☐ 1 cup of coffee
- ☐ 1 loaf French bread

Other

- ☐ _____
- ☐ _____
- ☐ _____
- ☐ _____
- ☐ _____
- ☐ _____
- ☐ _____
- ☐ _____

NOTES:

_____

_____

_____

_____

_____

_____

_____

_____

_____

_____

_____

_____

_____

NOTES:

Week Six Menu

PRESTO PASTA
AUNT JOAN'S FRUIT CUP

o

DELIGHTFULLY DIJON CHICKEN
SOUR CREAM PASTA

o

SUPER STROGANOFF SUPPER
SIMPLE SALAD

o

TURKEY AND STUFFING CASSEROLE

o

STAND-BY SPAGHETTI
CHOOSE-A-WAY BREADSTICKS

PRESTO PASTA

9 ounces uncooked angel hair pasta
3 cups broccoli florets, cooked
1 (10-ounce) jar of Alfredo Sauce (I like Five Brothers®)
1½ cups of diced or cubed ham, cooked
Parmesan cheese

Cook pasta in boiling water for 7 minutes. Drain. Add cooked broccoli and ham. Toss and cook another minute. Drain again. Add sauce and cook until heated through. Salt and pepper to taste. Serve onto plates and top with Parmesan cheese. Serve with Aunt Joan's Fruit Cup (below). Makes 6 servings.

AUNT JOAN'S FRUIT CUP

Your choice of fresh fruit, i.e. sliced peaches, sliced
    strawberries, blueberries, raspberries
Brown sugar
Sour Cream

Simply arrange fresh fruit in individual dessert bowls. Sprinkle each serving with brown sugar and then add a dollop of sour cream for an elegant yet simple dessert.

RUSH HOUR TIP:

Breadsticks always work well with pasta. You can purchase delicious Italian breadsticks in most grocery stores, or use a roll of breadstick dough from the refrigerator section of your local market. See Choose-A-Way Breadsticks (p. 202) for preparation ideas.

DELIGHTFULLY DIJON CHICKEN

½ cup dry bread crumbs
2 teaspoons Italian seasoning
½ teaspoon salt
½ teaspoon pepper
3 tablespoons Dijon-style mustard
6 chicken breasts
1 tablespoon olive oil

Combine first four ingredients in a shallow pan and mix well. Brush the mustard on both sides of each chicken breast and then dredge in seasoning mixture. Heat oil in a skillet over medium heat. Add chicken, cooking 6 minutes on each side or until cooked through. Serve with Sour Cream Pasta (below). Makes 6 servings.

SOUR CREAM PASTA

1 pound penne, cooked according to package directions
16 ounces low-fat sour cream
1 cup Parmesan cheese, divided

Preheat oven to 325 degrees. Toss sour cream and ½ cup of Parmesan cheese with the cooked pasta. Pour mixture into a 9 x13-inch baking dish coated with cooking spray. Top with the remaining Parmesan cheese. Bake for 30 minutes.

SUPER STROGANOFF SUPPER

According to *Cook's Illustrated*, the essential problem with stroganoff is that since it's made with a pan sauce, not as a slow braise or stew, it doesn't have time to develop that much flavor. Instead of slathering the meal with spices and extra ingredients to increase flavor, they offer a few simple tips...

- Cut beef tenderloin into thin strips—not thick
- Brown the mushrooms in pan before the beef
- Use white wine rather than red
- Consider adding a bit of chicken and/or beef broth in addition, or as a supplement to wine
- Use onions in place of shallots

I have incorporated these tips into the recipe below. You'll love this... and it's good for you, too! Who says great-tasting dishes can't be low in fat?

1½ pounds sirloin, cut into THIN strips
3 tablespoons flour
1 (12 ounce) jar of fat-free beef gravy
3 cloves minced garlic
½ teaspoon salt
¼ teaspoon sugar
¼ teaspoon pepper
1 cup of fresh mushrooms, sliced and sautéed
¾ cup sour cream (nonfat or low-fat)
½ bag of egg noodles

Cook egg noodles according to package directions. Sauté mushrooms; set aside. In the same nonstick skillet brown the sirloin strips. Sift flour into small bowl, add broth, and whisk well to avoid lumps. Add broth/flour mixture to skillet. Add garlic and seasonings. Continue stirring over low heat until meat is cooked. Add mushrooms and sour cream, stir until heated through and serve over noodles. Serve with Simple Salad (see page 64.) Makes 6 servings.

TURKEY AND STUFFING CASSEROLE

1 small onion, chopped
3 stalks of celery, chopped
3 cups of chicken broth (2 cups for first half of recipe, 1 cup
  for second part of recipe)
2 tablespoons flour
9 ounces of unseasoned stuffing-mix cubes
1½ pounds turkey breast, cut into strips
½ teaspoon thyme

Preheat oven to 350 degrees. Combine onion, celery and 2 cups of broth in a saucepan over medium heat. Cover and simmer until vegetables are soft. Add stuffing and thyme and mix well. Spray a 9 x 13-inch casserole dish and then spread vegetable mixture evenly along bottom of dish. Top with turkey strips. In a separate microwave-safe container, mix 1 cup broth with flour and whisk well. Cook mixture on high for 2-3 minutes, stirring occasionally. Pour mixture over turkey. Cover and bake for 25-30 minutes or until turkey is done and casserole is bubbly. Makes 6 servings.

STAND-BY SPAGHETTI

4 cups chicken broth
2 large eggs
2 cloves garlic, minced
¼ teaspoon pepper
2 (15 ounce) cans diced tomatoes, with juice
1 pound lean ground beef, turkey or veal, ground
½ cup bread crumbs
½ cup diced onion, optional
12 ounces tomato sauce
16 ounces spaghetti noodles

Beat eggs in a medium-size bowl. Add meat, pepper, garlic, bread crumbs, onion (if used) and enough chicken broth to moisten well (approximately ½ cup). Form meat mixture into meatballs. In a separate saucepan, warm water over medium heat. Drop meatballs into water. Cook for 5-8 minutes or until no longer pink Meanwhile, in a large saucepan combine remaining chicken broth, 2 cups water, tomatoes with juice and tomato sauce. Bring to a boil and then lower heat to a simmer. Remove meatballs from pot and add to tomato mixture. Bring to a boil. In a separate pot, cook pasta according to package directions. Serve with Choose-A-Way Breadsticks (see page 202). Makes 6 generous servings.

RUSH HOUR TIP:

Make Ahead Strategy: Omit onions and garlic from meatballs for a perfectly kid-friendly dish. Or better yet, make a multitude of meatballs as a make-ahead meal. Simply double or triple the recipe and then split into separate bowls. For the "adult" bowl, add all the extras. Place the assembled raw meatballs in a single layer on a cookie sheet and freeze. Once frozen, you can then place them all in a bag. Make sure to clearly label each bag so you remember which is yours and which one is Junior's. There is nothing like the trauma of "Junior" discovering an onion in his meatball, half-way through dinner! Pull meatballs from the freezer as you need them.

SUPER SAUCE

4 pounds Italian sausage, crumbled
3 medium onions, chopped
2 cups mushrooms, sliced
8 cloves garlic, minced
4 (14.5 ounce) cans diced tomatoes, still in liquid
2 (29 ounce) cans tomato sauce
2 (12 ounce) cans tomato paste
4 tablespoons dried basil
2 tablespoons sugar
1 teaspoon salt
1 teaspoon pepper

Cook sausage, onions, mushrooms and garlic over medium heat for about 8 minutes or until sausage is cooked through. Transfer mixture into a large pot or crockpot. Add remaining ingredients and stir well. Cook on low heat of stovetop for 4-5 hours, or in crockpot for 9-10 hours. Makes a ton.

RUSH HOUR TIP

Yes, this recipe makes a ton, but that's because I want you to keep your store-bought pasta jars and rinse them when empty.* Then fill them with this tasty homemade version. Provided you keep pasta in the pantry, you'll always be able to grab this homemade sauce from your freezer for a quick dinner. *Jars can be sterilized in dishwasher.

VEGETARIAN TIP

Omit the meat from this sauce recipe. Add more veggies to thicken the sauce

Week Six Grocery List

Produce

- ☐ 3 cups mushrooms
- ☐ 4 medium onions
- ☐ 13 cloves garlic
- ☐ 3 stalks celery
- ☐ 3 cups broccoli florets
- ☐ Choice of fresh fruit for fruit cup
- ☐ 1 head lettuce*
- ☐ 12 cherry tomatoes*
- ☐ 1 small red onion*
- ☐ ½ cup shredded carrot*

Canned/Boxed Goods

- ☐ 10 ounce jar of Alfredo Sauce(I use Five Brothers)
- ☐ Dijon-style mustard
- ☐ 6 cans diced tomatoes
- ☐ 2 (29 ounce) cans tomato sauce
- ☐ 2 (12 ounce) cans tomato paste
- ☐ 7 cups chicken broth
- ☐ 1 (12 ounce) jar of beef gravy
- ☐ 9 ounces unseasoned stuffing mix cubes
- ☐ Egg noodles
- ☐ Spaghetti noodles
- ☐ 1 pound penne pasta

Pantry/Spices

- ☐ Bread crumbs
- ☐ Italian seasoning
- ☐ Salt

- ☐ Pepper

- ☐ Olive oil
- ☐ Basil
- ☐ Sugar
- ☐ Thyme
- ☐ Flour
- ☐ Brown sugar

Meat

- ☐ 1½ cups diced or cubed ham
- ☐ 6 chicken breasts
- ☐ 4 pounds Italian sausage
- ☐ 1½ pounds turkey breast
- ☐ 1 pound lean ground beef, turkey or veal
- ☐ 1½ pounds sirloin

Dairy

- ☐ Parmesan cheese
- ☐ 2 eggs
- ☐ 2 large containers sour cream

Frozen

- ☐ 3 cups broccoli florets

Other

- ☐ Your choice of toppings for Choose-A-Way Breadsticks (see p. 202)
- ☐ 2 cans refrigerated breadstick dough
- ☐ Dressing for Simple Salad (or add the ingredients from one of the recipes on pages 29-32.)
- ☐ _____
- ☐ _____
- ☐ _____
- ☐ _____

☐ _____
☐ _____
☐ _____
☐ _____
☐ _____

*These ingredients are for the
Simple Salad Recipe (p. 64)

NOTES:

_____

_____

_____

_____

_____

_____

_____

_____

_____

_____

_____

_____

_____

_____

_____

_____

_____

_____

NOTES:

Week Seven Menu

POT ROAST PERFECTION
CINNAMON SWEET POTATOES

o

SHEPHERD'S PIE
SWEET AND SOUR CARROTS

o

MAGNIFICENT MAC
PRETTY PEACH CUP

o

COOL CRISPY CHICKEN
BAKED POTATO BONANZA

o

STEAK SOUP
SIMPLE SALAD

POT ROAST PERFECTION

1 (3 pound) beef roast
1 pound onions, sliced
1 (12 ounce) bottle of beer
1 package oxtail soup mix

In a large pan mix ⅛ cup water with onions and stir for 5
minutes. Transfer onions to crock pot. Add beer, soup mix and
1 cup water to crock pot and stir well. Place meat into mixture
and cook on low setting for 6-8 hours. Let stand 10 minutes
before serving. Serve with Cinnamon Sweet
Potatoes (below). Makes 12 servings.

Although the beer is absorbed in this recipe,
you can substitute beef broth if you like.

SHOULD YOU OPT FOR THE STOVE...

In the recipe above and other recipes that you choose to
convert from crock pot cooking, use a 325-degree oven.
For rare meat estimate 12-14 minutes per pound. For
medium increase average to 13-15 minute per pound.

CINNAMON SWEET POTATOES

3 large sweet potatoes, skin left on
2 teaspoons ground cinnamon

Scrub potatoes well and trim ends. Prick with a fork. Place
potatoes side by side on a paper towel in microwave oven.
Cook on high for 6-9 minutes, or until soft when pierced with
a fork. Sprinkle with cinnamon. Makes 6 servings.

SHEPHERD'S PIE

1 pound ground beef or turkey
⅛ cup red wine vinegar
2½ cups beef broth, divided
6 cups prepared mashed potatoes (instant is my choice!)
¼ cup horseradish
2 tablespoons cornstarch
1½ cup frozen peas
½ cup Cheddar cheese

Turn oven to broil setting. Brown the ground beef (or turkey) in a sauté pan. Drain off any excess fat and return to pan. Combine the meat with the vinegar and 1 cup broth over high heat. When the meat is fully cooked add cornstarch, peas and remaining broth. Bring to a boil and remove from heat. Transfer filling to a 12-inch ovenproof casserole dish. Combine horseradish and Cheddar cheese with the mashed potatoes and scoop around the edges of the casserole. Broil 7-10 minutes, or until potatoes are lightly browned and filling is warm and bubbly. Serve with Sweet and Sour Carrots below. Makes 6 servings.

SWEET & SOUR CARROTS

1 pound baby carrots
1½ tablespoons butter
¼ cup cider vinegar
⅓ cup sugar
1 tablespoon honey

Scrub carrots and cut into quarters lengthwise. Steam for 8 minutes or until crisp-tender. Drain and return carrots to pan. Add all other ingredients and warm over low heat until heated through. Makes 4 servings.

Most kids enjoy this dish, but if yours does not, just serve baby carrots raw with some dipping sauce.

MAGNIFICENT MAC

3 cups chicken broth
1½ cups skim milk
¾ pound elbow macaroni
1½ tablespoons cornstarch
1½ cups frozen peas
½ pound Canadian bacon, cubed
8 ounces Cheddar cheese, shredded

In a large saucepan bring broth, milk and macaroni to a boil. Cook for 10 minutes, stirring frequently. Blend cornstarch with 5 tablespoons of water. Stir into pan and continue stirring until mixture returns to a boil. Add peas and bacon; mix well and then remove from heat. Add cheese and stir for 1-2 more minutes to blend. Serve with Pretty Peach Cup (below). Makes 6 servings.

PRETTY PEACH CUP

1 pint strawberries, hulled
1 pint blueberries
4 peaches, pitted (or use canned)
½ teaspoon lemon juice
1 tablespoon sugar

Wash and drain all fruit. Slice fruit. Toss fruit with lemon juice. Sprinkle with sugar. Makes 4 servings.

RUSH HOUR TIP:

To slice fruit quickly and easily, use an egg slicer. This is also a great way to get a nice cut to use in party trays, as a garnish, etc.

COOL CRISPY CHICKEN

6 boneless chicken breasts
3 tablespoons flour
⅓ cup Dijon-style mustard
½ cup dry bread crumbs
Cooking oil

Coat rinsed chicken with flour. Spread mustard over flour then dredge in bread crumbs. Cook chicken in hot oil over medium heat 4 to 6 minutes on each side or until no longer pink. Serve with Baked Potato Bonanza (page 116). Makes 6 servings.

You can make any chicken breast meal more kid-friendly by simply cutting chicken breast into 1-inch strips, dredging in bread crumbs and cooking separately. Serve with ranch dressing or ketchup.

RUSH HOUR TIP:

Conquering Crinkly-Wrinkly Potatoes

To avoid cracked and wrinkled skins on your baked potatoes spread a small amount of oil on the outside of the potato before baking.

BAKED POTATO BONANZA

6 potatoes
Vegetable oil

Preheat oven to 400 degrees. Scrub potatoes and blot dry with a paper towel. Rub oil on skins to avoid cracking. Pierce potatoes twice with a fork. For soft-skinned potatoes, wrap in aluminum foil. For crispier skins, do not use foil. Bake for 1 hour in or until soft when gently squeezed.

Baked potatoes are often thought of as an accompaniment but they can also make a wonderful main meal! Just add some veggies and some protein. Serve baked potatoes with a "Bonanza Bar" of toppings. Let each person "dress" his or her potato according to their tastes.

Bacon bits (or crumbled bacon)   Canned mushrooms
Green onions, chopped   Onions, diced
Broccoli florets, steamed   Parmesan cheese
Cheddar cheese, shredded   Swiss cheese, shredded
Cubed ham   Ground beef, cooked
Sour cream   Yogurt
Ground turkey   Cheese sauce
Any cheese

To microwave 2 potatoes, prick with fork and cook 10-12 minutes or until soft to the touch.

STEAK SOUP

4 (4 ounce) beef steaks, cubed
½ teaspoon garlic salt
½ teaspoon pepper
1 cup chopped onion
½ cup chopped celery
4 cups water
1 (10 ounce) package frozen mixed vegetables
1 tablespoon beef bouillon granules
1 tablespoon Worcestershire sauce
1 (7.5 ounce) can diced tomatoes, in liquid
½ cup water
⅓ cup flour

Sprinkle meat with garlic salt and pepper. Cook meat in a tad of oil over medium heat for 3 minutes, or until done. Remove and reserve. Add onion and celery to meat drippings and cook until tender. Return meat to pan along with water, frozen veggies, bouillon and Worcestershire sauce. Bring to a boil, then reduce heat. Cover and simmer 5-8 minutes or until veggies are tender. Stir in tomatoes and liquid. Mix ½ cup water and flour well. Add to soup mixture and stir to mix thoroughly. Continue cooking until thick and bubbly. Serve with Simple Salad (see page 64). Makes 4-6 servings.

RUSH HOUR TIP:

Spice Primer
Stuck on which spice to choose?
Here are a few simple guidelines…
Beef: Rosemary, basil, garlic, onion powder
Pork: sage, garlic, chives, basil, marjoram, oregano
Chicken: sage, basil, marjoram, thyme
Fish: sage, fennel, dill, basil and parsley

Grocery List Week Seven

Produce

- [ ] 1 pound +2 onions
- [ ] ½ cup of celery
- [ ] 3 large sweet potatoes
- [ ] 1 pound baby carrots
- [ ] 6 baking potatoes
- [ ] 1 pint strawberries
- [ ] 1 pint blueberries
- [ ] 4 fresh peaches
- [ ] 1 head lettuce*
- [ ] 1 small red onion*
- [ ] 12 cherry tomatoes*
- [ ] ½ cup shredded carrots*

Canned/Boxed Goods

- [ ] Dijon-style mustard
- [ ] Worcestershire sauce
- [ ] 1 (7.5) ounce can diced tomatoes
- [ ] 1 package oxtail soup mix
- [ ] 2½ cups beef broth
- [ ] 6 cups prepared mashed potatoes
- [ ] Prepared horseradish
- [ ] 3 cups chicken broth
- [ ] Elbow macaroni
- [ ] Beef bouillon granules

Pantry/Spices

- [ ] Dry bread crumbs
- [ ] Vegetable oil
- [ ] Cooking oil
- [ ] Flour
- [ ] Garlic salt
- [ ] Cinnamon
- [ ] Pepper
- [ ] Cornstarch

- [ ] Red wine vinegar
- [ ] Cider Vinegar
- [ ] Sugar

Meat

- [ ] 6 boneless chicken breasts
- [ ] 4 (4 ounce) beef steaks
- [ ] 3 pound beef roast
- [ ] 1 pound ground beef or turkey
- [ ] ½ pound Canadian bacon

Dairy

- [ ] 1½ cups skim milk
- [ ] Butter
- [ ] 2½ cups Cheddar cheese

Frozen

- [ ] 10 ounce package of frozen mixed vegetables
- [ ] 3 cups frozen peas

Miscellaneous

- [ ] 1 bottle of beer
- [ ] Honey
- [ ] Lemon juice

Other

- [ ] Toppings for baked potatoes (see baked potato Bonanza, pg. 116)
- [ ] Dressing* of choice (or use recipe from page 29-32).
- [ ] _____
- [ ] _____
- [ ] _____
- [ ] _____

- ❏ _____
- ❏ _____
- ❏ _____
- ❏ _____
- ❏ _____
- ❏ _____

- ❏ _____
- ❏ _____
- ❏ _____

*These ingredients are for the Simple Salad (p. 64) side dish.

NOTES:

_____

_____

_____

_____

_____

_____

_____

_____

_____

_____

_____

_____

_____

_____

_____

_____

_____

_____

_____

_____

NOTES:

_____

_____

_____

_____

_____

_____

_____

_____

_____

_____

_____

_____

_____

_____

_____

_____

_____

_____

_____

_____

_____

HONEY CHOPS
TWICE AS NICE VEGGIE RICE

o

BOWTIE BONANZA
TOMATO BREAD

o

SPEEDY SALISBURY STEAK
RANCH POTATOES

o

CHICKEN AND VEGETABLE BAKE
I-SLAVED-ALL-DAY BISCUITS

o

CHICKEN FETTUCCINI DIJON
AWESOME APPLESAUCE

HONEY CHOPS

6 bone-in pork chops
⅓ cup honey
⅓ cup lemon juice
3 tablespoons soy sauce
3 garlic cloves, minced

Cook chops in a skillet over medium heat for 10-15 minutes or until done. Remove and keep warm. Add other ingredients to pan and heat for 3-5 minutes. Pour over chops. Serve with Twice as Nice Veggie Rice (page 123). Makes 6 servings.

RUSH HOUR TIP

I am a big fan of French or special breads with dinner. If a loaf is too large for your family or you have leftovers, bread can be reheated successfully. Wrap bread in a dampened towel and bake for several minutes in a 350-degree oven to help retain moisture. After bread has been reheated once, it usually won't survive another heating. In that case, slice bread, butter and season with your choice of seasonings. Broil until lightly browned. Store these in airtight containers as snacks; use as croutons in salads; or garnish for soups and stews.

TWICE AS NICE VEGGIE RICE

2 cups bean sprouts
1 cup shredded carrots
1 teaspoon ginger root
3 garlic cloves, minced
1½ cups sliced mushrooms
2-3 tablespoons oil, divided
3 cups long-grain white rice, cooked
⅛ cup soy sauce
1 cup frozen peas, thawed
½ cup sliced green onions, tops included

In a little oil cook sprouts, carrots, ginger, garlic and
mushrooms over medium heat for a minute or two. Remove
from pan and set aside. Heat remaining oil and then add
cooked rice and soy sauce. Cook 3-5 minutes. Add sprout
mixture, along with peas and onions back into pan. Stir
gently. Cook until heated through. Serve
alongside Honey Chops. (previous page)
Makes 6 servings.

For kids, keep some of the rice separate!

RUSH HOUR TIP:

Did you know that you can dice onions and peppers in
advance and store them in your freezer for up to one
month? This is a great way to make dinner prep a breeze!

BOWTIE BONANZA

8 ounces bowtie pasta
3 garlic cloves, minced
2 tablespoons butter
¼ cup green onions,
   (adult portions only)

½ pound mushrooms, sliced
½ cup Parmesan cheese
2 tablespoons oil

Cook pasta according to package directions. Drain and toss with oil. Melt butter in skillet. Cook mushrooms and garlic for 2-3 minutes. Pour over pasta. Toss well. Serve onto plates and top with Parmesan cheese. Top with sliced green onions (on adult portions.) Serve with Tomato Bread (below). Makes 6 servings

Remember to be creative for kids. In this recipe you could remove a portion of the pasta, toss with butter and their cheese of choice. Serve with applesauce or fruit, a vegetable and a slice of French bread. For more protein, add cooked and shredded chicken or turkey.

TOMATO BREAD

½ loaf French bread
2 fresh tomatoes, chopped
1 tablespoon olive oil
1 tablespoon oregano
Sprinkling of Parmesan cheese

Preheat broiler. Cut French bread into 8 (1-inch) slices. Place bread on a baking sheet and broil 1-2 minutes on each side or until lightly browned. Meanwhile, combine tomatoes, oil and oregano is a small bowl. Remove bread from broiler and spread tomato mixture on bread. Sprinkle with Parmesan cheese. Makes 8 servings.

If your kids aren't tomato fans, melt cheese on their bread slices.

SPEEDY SALISBURY STEAK

1 pound ground round
1 egg
½ cup dry bread crumbs
½ cup milk
1 can cream of mushroom soup, divided
¼ teaspoon pepper
¼ cup onion, minced
¼ teaspoon salt
1 cup sliced mushrooms

Combine egg, bread crumbs, ⅓ of the soup and onion. Knead mixture into beef with hands. Form into 6 patties. Brown on both sides in a skillet over medium heat. Mix all remaining ingredients in a bowl and pour over patties. Cook 15-20 minutes or until done. Serve with Ranch Potatoes (below). Makes 6 servings.

RUSH HOUR TIP

Kitchen Caddies ~ Try using a carry-all caddie in your refrigerator! These inexpensive storage solutions can often be found at dollar-stores. They offer a great way to corral miscellaneous condiments together.

RANCH POTATOES

6 medium potatoes
2 tablespoons olive oil
1 teaspoon paprika
1 teaspoon chopped parsley
1 teaspoon pepper
1 teaspoon garlic powder
1 package dry ranch-dressing mix

Preheat oven to 425 degrees. Cut potatoes into quarters and then into thirds (you should end up with 72 potato pieces). Mix all the dry seasonings together. Place oil, spices and potatoes into a zipper-top bag and shake to coat. Place in a single layer on a baking sheet. Bake for 40-45 minutes or until tender and golden brown. Makes 8-10 servings.

CHICKEN AND VEGETABLE BAKE

6 ounces long grain wild rice
1 can cream of mushroom soup
6 boneless, skinless chicken breasts
⅛ teaspoon each salt and pepper
1 package frozen peas and carrots mixture

Preheat oven to 350 degrees. Mix all ingredients except chicken in a bowl. Pour into a baking dish. Top with chicken. Cover and bake 40-45 minutes in or until chicken is no longer pink and rice is tender. Serve with I-Slaved-All-Day Biscuits (below). Makes 6 servings.

I-SLAVED-ALL-DAY CHEDDAR AND HERB BISCUITS

1 tube of refrigerated biscuits
3 tablespoons butter or margarine
1 tablespoon mixed garlic powder, pepper and dill (or
    mixed seasonings of your choice)
1 cup shredded Cheddar cheese

Preheat oven to 375 degrees or as directed on biscuit package. Melt butter and mix with seasonings. Brush over the biscuits and top with a pinch of Cheddar cheese. Bake for 12 minutes or as directed on the package. You can serve these biscuits without butter, as they are tasty enough as is. Makes 8 servings.

My friend tells a great story about her mother, who may possibly be my match in level of cooking skills. For her daughter's prom party she decided to bake. The basis of each appetizer was Rhodes® bread dough! She had a spread of 10-15 appetizers—Rhodes® dough baked every which way! Just goes to show the versatility of bread dough.

CHICKEN FETTUCCINI DIJON

1 cup fat-free sour cream
2 tablespoons Dijon-style mustard
4 boneless, skinless chicken breasts
½ pound mushrooms, sliced
6 ounces fettuccini
Salt and pepper to taste

Prepare fettuccini according to package directions. Stir sour cream and mustard together in a small bowl. Spray a skillet with cooking spray. Cook chicken breasts over medium heat, 8-10 minutes, or until chicken is cooked through and no longer pink. Remove chicken and cover to keep warm. Add mushrooms and a bit of water into skillet. Cover and cook over medium heat until soft, 2-3 minutes. Add sour-cream/mustard mixture to mushrooms and heat, being careful not to boil. Return chicken to skillet and gently mix all together. Divide fettuccini equally on serving plates and top with chicken mixture. Salt and pepper to taste. Serve with Awesome Applesauce (below). Makes 4 servings.

AWESOME APPLESAUCE

6 apples
¼ cup water
1 teaspoon cinnamon
½ cup sugar or to taste
2½ tablespoons brown sugar

Core, peel and slice apples. Simmer apples in water for 15-20 minutes or until apples are tender. Remove from heat. Mash apples slightly and add cinnamon and sugar. Sample. If you would like sweeter applesauce, add more sugar. Makes 6 servings.

Grocery List Week Eight

Produce

- 2 pounds sliced mushrooms (32 ounces)
- 1 cup shredded carrots
- 9 cloves garlic
- 1 bunch green onions
- 2 cups bean sprouts
- Ginger root (fresh or bottled)
- 1 onion
- 6 medium potatoes
- 2 tomatoes
- 6 apples

Canned/Boxed Goods

- 2 cans cream of mushroom soup
- 1 package dry ranch dressing mix
- 6 ounces long grain wild rice
- Soy sauce
- Honey
- 3 cups long-grain white rice
- 8 ounces bow-tie pasta
- Dijon-style mustard
- 6 ounces fettuccini noodles

Pantry/Spices

- Garlic powder
- Dill
- Pepper
- Bread crumbs
- Salt
- Paprika

- Olive oil
- Parsley
- Lemon juice
- Oregano
- Cinnamon
- Sugar
- Brown sugar
- Vegetable oil

Meat

- 1 pound ground round
- 10 boneless, skinless chicken breasts
- 6 bone-in pork chops

Dairy

- Butter
- 1 tube refrigerated biscuits
- 8 ounces Cheddar cheese
- 1 egg
- ½ cup milk
- ½ cup Parmesan cheese
- 1 cup sour cream

Frozen

- 1 cup frozen peas
- 1 package frozen pea and carrot mixture
- 1 loaf French bread

Other

- _____
- _____
- _____
- _____

Week Nine Menu

TASTY TURKEY SLICES
BREADED MOZZARELLA STICKS

○

TURKEY POT PIE
BERRY COMPOTE

○

LASAGNA ROLLS
BEDAZZLING BREADSTICKS

○

ROCKIN' ROTINI
ROSEMARY BROCCOLI

○

CHICKEN PARMESAN
AUNT SALLY'S POTATOES

TASTY-TURKEY SLICES

6 thick turkey breast slices   2 eggs
3 tablespoons milk   2 cups Italian dry bread crumbs
½ cup butter

Beat eggs and milk together. Dip turkey slices in egg mixture
then dredge in bread crumbs. Melt butter in skillet over
medium heat. Brown turkey 2-4 minutes per side, or until
juices run clear. Serve with Baked Mozzarella Sticks (below).
Makes 6 servings.

BAKED MOZZARELLA STICKS

2 eggs
1 tablespoon water
1 cup Italian dry bread crumbs
1 teaspoon garlic powder
¼ teaspoon pepper
½ cup crushed corn flakes
½ cup flour
12 sticks string cheese
1 cup prepared spaghetti sauce, for dipping (like Ragu®)

Preheat oven to 400 degrees. Beat eggs and water in a small
bowl. In a separate bowl, mix bread crumbs, garlic powder,
pepper and crushed corn flakes. Place flour in a separate
bowl. Dip each stick of cheese into flour, then egg, and then
dredge in bread crumb mixture. Place on ungreased baking
sheet, cover and freeze for one hour before cooking. Bake
(uncovered) for 7-9 minutes or until golden and crisp. Serve
with spaghetti sauce for dipping. Makes 4 servings.

TURKEY POT PIE

1 (10.5 ounce) can cream of chicken soup
1 (10.5 ounce) can cream of potato soup
1 "soup can" skim milk
1 thick turkey breast, cooked and shredded or 2-3 cups
   leftover turkey meat
2 cups frozen peas and carrots, cooked and drained
3-4 potatoes, peeled, cubed and drained
1 onion, diced finely
2 packages refrigerated biscuits
1 teaspoon salt
½ teaspoon pepper
½ teaspoon celery flakes
½ teaspoon parsley flakes

In a 9 x 13-inch casserole-baking dish, combine soups with milk and seasonings. Break up turkey into bite-sized pieces and stir into soups. Add cooked peas and carrots, potatoes and the fresh onion. Bake at 400 degrees for 20 minutes. Remove casserole dish from oven and place biscuits on top of the turkey and vegetable mixture. Cover entire dish with the biscuits. Return dish to oven, reduce heat to 350 degrees and bake until the biscuit topping is golden brown—about 20-25 minutes. Serve with Berry Compote (132). Makes 6 servings.

FIVE-A-DAY CONTEST

If you want to try to encourage fruit and veggie consumption in your home, try a five-a-day contest. Put each person's name on a chart on the fridge. Tack up a list of "serving" sizes (i.e. ½ banana = 1 fruit, 1 small apple = 1 fruit, ½ cup carrots = 1 vegetable) see who can eat the most each day and let the winner of the week choose a special meal. (You can do this same style competition with water consumption.) Of course, it's not the competition that we're after, but the habit of observing how much of the good-raw-stuff we actually eat in a day!

BERRY COMPOTE

1 pint strawberries, hulled, washed and sliced
1 cup blackberries, rinsed
1 cup blueberries, rinsed
1 cup raspberries, rinsed
½ cup fat-free whipped topping (such as Cool Whip®)

Gently toss all berries together in a large bowl. Divide fruit among serving bowls. Top with a dollop of whipped topping. Chill. Makes 4 servings.

LASAGNA ROLLS

1 pound ground turkey or beef
1 (16 ounce) container cottage cheese
2 cups mozzarella cheese, divided
1 tablespoon minced garlic
1 tablespoon oregano
1 (24 ounce) jar of prepared spaghetti sauce
1 package lasagna noodles

Preheat oven to 350 degrees. Prepare noodles according to package directions, set aside. Mix cottage cheese and 1 cup mozzarella cheese, set aside. Brown ground turkey or beef with garlic and oregano. Place ⅛ cup ground meat mixture on each noodle and spread cheese mixture over meat. Roll and place in 9 x 13-inch baking pan. Repeat process with each noodle. Pour spaghetti sauce over noodle-rolls and sprinkle with remaining cheese. Bake covered for 35-45 minutes or until sauce is bubbly and cheese has melted. Serve with Bedazzling Breadsticks (page 133). Makes 6 servings.

RUSH HOUR TIP

Make extra "rolls" and freeze them in aluminum foil. To serve for dinner, transfer to refrigerator the night before cooking. Warm until heated through in a 325-degree oven.

BEDAZZLING BREADSTICKS

1 can refrigerated biscuits
1 tablespoon garlic powder
2 tablespoons butter, melted
1 tablespoon sesame seeds
1 tablespoon poppy seeds
1 tablespoon dried minced onion

Preheat oven according to biscuit package directions. Roll biscuits into 5 to 6-inch long breadstick shapes. Mix garlic powder and melted butter in small bowl. Brush onto breadsticks. Sprinkle with sesame seeds, poppy seeds and minced onion. Bake according to package directions. Makes 8 servings.

CONQUER KITCHEN CLUTTER

*Use caddies to round up like items such as condiments, cooking utensils, cleaning supplies, etc.

*Assign each family member a drawer. Teach them that if they want to have something in the kitchen it should go in their drawer—not on your counter!

*Take stock of your cabinets. Do you have dishes you hardly ever use taking up valuable space? Consider transferring these dishes to another closet or store carefully in crates.

*Twice a year, go through all your cabinets and take out any non-perishables you haven't eaten during the past 6 months. Donate these items to a food drive.

ROCKIN' ROTINI

12 ounces tri-colored rotini pasta
1 cup diced deli salami
1 cup diced provolone cheese
1 cup fat-free Italian salad dressing

Cook rotini according to package
directions, drain and rinse with cold
water. Add all other ingredients and
toss to mix. Cover and refrigerate until
serving. Serve with Rosemary Broccoli
(below). Makes 6 servings.

ROSEMARY BROCCOLI

1 teaspoon dried rosemary (or 1 tablespoon fresh)
2 pounds broccoli, rinsed and cut into bite-sized pieces
1 teaspoon lemon juice

Bring 2 inches of water to a boil. Add rosemary to boiling
water and reduce heat to a simmer. Place broccoli into a
steaming basket and cook covered, for 5 minutes or until
crisp-tender. Transfer broccoli to a serving bowl and toss with
lemon juice. Makes 6 servings.

KITCHEN STRATEGIES

Make sure your dishwasher is empty before you start
dinner preparations. This way you can transfer used dishes
to the dishwasher as you go and avoid a pile to clean up
later! Also fill your sink with hot, soapy water. Wipe down
countertops as you go to avoid dried and crusty foods that
need to be scrubbed off! Cooking becomes a lot easier when
we get the "clean-up" under control. You can also try my
favorite method—whoever cooks, doesn't clean. Let those
who enjoy the meal share in the clean-up, too!

CHICKEN PARMESAN

4 skinless, boneless chicken breasts
½ cup flour
1 tablespoon oregano
1 tablespoon garlic, if desired
½ cup Parmesan cheese, divided
1 jar spaghetti sauce (I prefer meatless)
1 (8 ounce) package shredded mozzarella cheese
Cooking spray
4 cups cooked pasta, your choice

Preheat oven to 375 degrees. Rinse chicken breasts and set aside. Mix flour, oregano, garlic and ¼ cup of the Parmesan cheese in a shallow bowl. Coat chicken with this mixture. Spray pan with cooking spray and cook chicken until golden brown on both sides. After chicken is browned, transfer to baking dish and cover with sauce and remaining ¼ cup of Parmesan cheese. Bake, covered for 30 minutes. Uncover and top with mozzarella cheese and cook for an additional 10 minutes or until bubbly. Serve with your favorite pasta or serve with Aunt Sally's Potatoes (below). Makes 4 servings.

AUNT SALLY'S POTATOES

1 red onion sliced
1 (32 ounce) package of frozen hash browns
1 (8 ounce) container of sour cream
1 (8 ounce) package of shredded Cheddar cheese
1 can of cream of chicken soup
2 tablespoons butter
1 teaspoon garlic powder
1 can Durkee's® Fried Onion Rings

Preheat oven to 350 degrees. Mix first 7 ingredients together and place in a casserole dish. Bake covered for 60 minutes. Let stand for 15 minutes. Top with one can of Durkee's™ fried onions and bake for an additional 10-15 minutes, uncovered, until browned and bubbly. Makes 8 servings.

Grocery List Week Nine

Produce

- [ ] 1 red onion
- [ ] 1 onion
- [ ] 3-4 potatoes
- [ ] 2 pounds broccoli
- [ ] 1 pint strawberries
- [ ] 1 cup blueberries
- [ ] 1 cup blackberries
- [ ] 1 cup raspberries
- [ ] 1 jar minced garlic

Deli

- [ ] 1 cup deli diced salami

Canned/Boxed Goods

- [ ] Corn flakes
- [ ] 3 jars spaghetti sauce
- [ ] 2 cans cream of chicken soup
- [ ] 1 can Durkee® fried onion rings
- [ ] 1 can cream of potato soup
- [ ] 1 package lasagna noodles
- [ ] 1 (12 ounce) package tri-colored rotini pasta
- [ ] 4 cups cooked pasta, your choice
- [ ] Fat-free Italian dressing
- [ ] Lemon juice
- [ ] Parmesan cheese
- [ ] Cooking spray

Pantry/Spices

- [ ] Italian dry bread crumbs
- [ ] Garlic powder
- [ ] Pepper
- [ ] Flour
- [ ] Salt
- [ ] Celery flakes
- [ ] Parsley flakes
- [ ] Oregano
- [ ] Sesame seeds
- [ ] Poppy seeds
- [ ] Dried minced onion
- [ ] Dried rosemary

Meat

- [ ] 6 thick turkey breast slices
- [ ] 1 thick turkey breast
- [ ] 4 boneless, skinless chicken breasts
- [ ] 1 pound ground turkey or beef
- [ ] 8 ounces deli salami

Dairy

- [ ] Milk
- [ ] Butter
- [ ] 4 eggs
- [ ] 12 sticks string cheese
- [ ] 3 packages refrigerated biscuits
- [ ] 1 (16 ounce) container cottage cheese
- [ ] 3 cups shredded mozzarella cheese
- [ ] 1 cup provolone cheese, diced
- [ ] 1 (8 ounce) container sour cream
- [ ] 1 (8 ounce) package of shredded Cheddar cheese
- [ ] Fat-free whipped topping

Frozen

- ☐ 1 (32 ounce) package of frozen hash browns
- ☐ 2 cups pea and carrot mixture

Other

- ☐ _____
- ☐ _____
- ☐ _____
- ☐ _____
- ☐ _____
- ☐ _____

- ☐ _____
- ☐ _____
- ☐ _____
- ☐ _____
- ☐ _____
- ☐ _____
- ☐ _____
- ☐ _____
- ☐ _____
- ☐ _____
- ☐ _____
- ☐ _____
- ☐ _____
- ☐ _____

NOTES:

_____

_____

_____

_____

_____

_____

_____

_____

_____

_____

_____

_____

_____

_____

NOTES:

Week Ten Menu

HAM AND POTATOES
GLORIOUS GREEN BEANS

○

STACKED CHOPS WITH
BAKED POTATO BONANZA

○

HAMMY NOODLES
GLORIOUS GREEN BEANS

○

NO RED-SAUCE SPAGHETTI
BEDAZZLING BREADSTICKS
SIMPLE SALAD

○

GRILLED HONEY-CHICKEN
EASY PASTA TOSS

HAM AND POTATOES

10 medium potatoes, peeled and sliced
1 teaspoon salt
½ teaspoon pepper
1 onion, chopped
2 pounds baked ham, cut in thin strips or diced into small
  squares
1 package instant dry onion soup mix
1 can cream of mushroom soup
1 soup can water
2 cups shredded Cheddar cheese
1 cup American processed cheese spread

Combine all ingredients in a crockpot and mix well. Cover with
lid and cook on low setting for 6 hours or until potatoes are
tender. Serve with Glorious Green Beans (page 86). Makes 8
servings.

STACKED CHOPS

8 thin, boneless pork chops
1 package prepared Stove Top™
  stuffing
1 package frozen mixed veggies
¼ cup water
1 can cream of mushroom soup

Preheat oven to 375 degrees. Place
frozen veggies in bottom of 9 x 13-
inch casserole dish. Layer 4 chops on
top of veggies. Place prepared
stuffing on top of chops. Layer next 4
chops on top of stuffing mix. Mix
canned soup with ¼ cup water and
pour over top. Bake for 35-45 minutes or until chops are done.
Serve with Baked Potato Bonanza (page 116). Makes 4
servings.

HAMMY NOODLES

¾ pound ham, diced
1½ cups shredded cheese (you choose the type: Parmesan,
  mozzarella, Swiss or Cheddar)
1½ cup light cream
1¼ pound linguine

Cook pasta according to package directions. Rinse, drain and
reserve in a serving bowl. Warm cream over low heat. Once
hot, add ham and continue cooking for 5-10 minutes, stirring
frequently. Do not boil. Add cheese. Stir until melted, and
sauce thickens. Mix sauce with pasta in a serving bowl. Tada!
Serve with Glorious Green Beans (page 86). Makes 6 servings.

NO-RED-SAUCE SPAGHETTI

1 pound spaghetti   ½ pound bacon, diced
½ cup frozen peas   ½ cup frozen corn
½ pound pre-sliced pepper-
  oni, cut in halves

Cook bacon and pepperoni over medium heat until bacon is
crisp. Cook pasta according to package directions, drain. Cook
corn and peas according to package directions, drain. Mix
vegetables and meats (with their drippings) with pasta. Toss
and serve. Serve with Bedazzling Breadsticks (page 133) and
Simple Salad (see page 64) Makes 4 servings.

GRILLED HONEY CHICKEN

1 tablespoon orange juice
2 teaspoons lemon juice
2 teaspoons honey
2 teaspoons reduced-sodium soy sauce
2 garlic cloves, minced
4 boneless, skinless chicken breasts

Combine all ingredients except chicken and whisk until well-blended. Add chicken breasts to mixture, turning several times to coat. Cover dish with plastic wrap and let marinate 15-60 minutes in refrigerator. While meat is marinating, prepare grill. Grill 4-5 minutes per side or until chicken is no longer pink. If it's too cold to grill, bake in a 350-degree oven for 30-40 minutes or until chicken is no longer pink. Serve with Easy Pasta Toss (see page 61). Makes 4 servings.

VARIETY IS THE SPICE OF LIFE

The best meals are those that contain variety. Check your meals against the list below for maximum affect...

Variety in nutrition ~ Mix carbos and veggies. Despite all the fad diets, research still shows that the majority of our calories should come from carbs (about 55-60% percent) and 30-35% should come from protein.

Variety in texture – Pair crunchy foods with soft foods and crispier foods with tender foods. The contrast in texture helps accentuate each food more.

Variety in taste – Try serving the spicy with bland, or sweet foods with sour foods. Combinations of flavors enhance one another.

Variety in temperature – Serve a hot dish with a cold dish for maximum contrast and flavor.

Week Ten Grocery List

Produce
- ❑ 2 onions
- ❑ 10 medium potatoes
- ❑ 2 pounds green beans*
- ❑ 2 garlic cloves

Canned/Boxed Goods
- ❑ 1 package instant dry onion soup mix
- ❑ 2 cans cream of mushroom soup
- ❑ 1 package Stove Top® stuffing
- ❑ 1 pound spaghetti
- ❑ Soy sauce

Pantry/Spices
- ❑ Honey
- ❑ Salt
- ❑ Pepper
- ❑ Red wine vinegar*
- ❑ ¼ cup slivered almonds*

Meat
- ❑ 2¾ pounds baked ham
- ❑ 8 thin, boneless pork chops
- ❑ ½ pound bacon
- ❑ ½ pound pre-sliced pepperoni
- ❑ 4 boneless chicken breasts

Dairy
- ❑ 1 tablespoon orange juice
- ❑ 2 teaspoons lemon juice
- ❑ 2 cups shredded Cheddar cheese
- ❑ 1½ cups shredded cheese of your choice (for Hammy Noodles)
- ❑ 1½ cup light cream
- ❑ 1 cup American processed cheese spread

Frozen
- ❑ 1 package frozen mixed veggies
- ❑ ½ cup frozen peas
- ❑ ½ cup frozen corn

Other
- ❑ _____
- ❑ _____
- ❑ _____
- ❑ _____
- ❑ _____
- ❑ _____
- ❑ _____
- ❑ _____
- ❑ _____
- ❑ _____
- ❑ _____
- ❑ _____
- ❑ _____
- ❑ _____
- ❑ _____

Suggested Sides

The following side dishes
are suggested for this week's
recipes. Should you opt to use
them you will need to add
the ingredients to your
grocery list. All other listed
recipes are included in your
grocery list. If you choose to
use one of the Dazzling
Dressings (pages 29-32) you
will need to add the
ingredients to your shopping
list also.

BEDAZZLING BREADSTICKS
(recipe on p. 133 serve with
No Red-Sauce Spaghetti on p.
141)

EASY PASTA TOSS (recipe on
p. 61 serve with Grilled
Honey-Chicken on p. 142)

SIMPLE SALAD (recipe on p.
64 – serve with No Red-Sauce
Spaghetti on p. 141)

BAKED POTATO BONANZA
(recipe on p. 116 – serve with
Stacked Chops p. 140)

- ❑ _____
- ❑ _____
- ❑ _____
- ❑ _____
- ❑ _____
- ❑ _____
- ❑ _____
- ❑ _____
- ❑ _____
- ❑ _____
- ❑ _____
- ❑ _____
- ❑ _____
- ❑ _____
- ❑ _____
- ❑ _____
- ❑ _____
- ❑ _____
- ❑ _____
- ❑ _____
- ❑ _____
- ❑ _____
- ❑ _____
- ❑ _____
- ❑ _____
- ❑ _____
- ❑ _____
- ❑ _____
- ❑ _____
- ❑ _____

PERFECT PARMESAN CHICKEN
PERFECT PARMESAN POTATOES

○

ITALIAN CHICKEN IN A FLASH
ROBUST RICE PILAF

○

KIDS-LOVE-IT CASSEROLE
SIMPLE SALAD

○

TACO PIZZA

○

CHEESE PIZZA PLEASE

PERFECT PARMESAN CHICKEN

4 boneless skinless chicken breasts
1 cup bread crumbs
1 teaspoon salt
½ cup shredded Parmesan cheese

¾ cup Miracle Whip™
1 tablespoon oregano
1 tablespoon pepper

Preheat oven to 350 degrees. Mix bread crumbs, cheese, salt, pepper and oregano. Brush chicken with Miracle Whip™ and coat with crumb mixture. Bake in a 9 x 13-inch baking dish for 45 minutes or until golden brown and chicken is cooked through. Serve with Perfect Parmesan Potatoes (below). Makes 4 servings.

PERFECT PARMESAN POTATOES

4 cups mashed potatoes
⅓ cup milk
¼ cup Parmesan cheese

½ cup sour cream
¼ cup green onions*
Salt and pepper to taste

Blend all ingredients thoroughly. Broil 4-6 minutes or until heated through and lightly browned.

You may want to use the green onions as a garnish on adult servings to avoid contemptuous glances from youngsters.

ITALIAN CHICKEN IN A FLASH

1 cup Italian dressing
6 chicken breasts
⅛ cup shredded Parmesan cheese
2 tablespoons olive oil

Pound chicken breasts to ¼-inch thickness. Marinate in Italian dressing for 15 minutes. Sauté in olive oil over medium heat or until no longer pink, turning once, approximately 12-15 minutes. Sprinkle with Parmesan cheese. Serve with Robust Rice Pilaf (below). Makes 6 servings

RUSH HOUR TIP:

Italian dressing makes a great "instant" marinade. Customize store-bought dressing by adding a few of your own special touches. You may also want to try some of the dressings on page 29 or marinades on page 33.

ROBUST RICE PILAF

2 (14.5 ounce) cans chicken broth	½ cup water
2 cups uncooked long-grain rice	3 cloves garlic, minced
1 cup frozen peas	½ cup Parmesan cheese
⅓ cup green onions	Salt and pepper to taste

In a saucepan, sauté garlic over medium heat. Add rice. Cook 2 minutes, stirring constantly. Add water and broth and bring to a boil. Cover and reduce heat. Cook for 20 minutes or until liquid is absorbed. Fluff rice with a fork and then add peas, Parmesan cheese, green onions, salt and pepper. Toss well and serve. Makes 6 servings.

For truly picky-eaters, reserve some plain rice!

KIDS-LOVE-IT CASSEROLE

Kids may be my biggest fans, so every once in a while I feel obligated to put in a recipe purely for their benefit. Kids-Love-It Casserole is one such favorite. Have teens? They can make this on their own. Adults: use this as a base for taco salad and simply substitute fresh lettuce in place of the pizza crust!

1 pound ground beef
1 (15 ounce) can chunky tomato sauce
1 can refrigerated pizza crust dough
1½ cups mozzarella cheese, shredded

Preheat oven to 425 degrees. Cook meat until browned. Add sauce and cook until heated through. Meanwhile, press pizza dough into a 9 x 13-inchbaking dish. Sprinkle ½ cup of cheese over dough. Add meat mixture. Bake for 10-15 minutes. Add remaining cheese and cook an additional 5 minutes or until cheese is melted. Serve with Simple Salad (page 64). Make 6 servings.

TACO PIZZA

1 tube refrigerated pizza dough
½ pound ground beef
1 cup shredded mozzarella cheese

4 ounces pizza sauce
½ taco seasoning packet

Preheat oven to 400 degrees. Brown beef in skillet coated with cooking spray and season with ½ of the taco seasoning packet. Spread sauce over pizza dough and top with beef, then mozzarella cheese. Bake for 15-20 minutes and then cut into squares and serve. Add a tossed salad to get in your vegetables!

CHEESE PIZZA PLEASE

1 (10 ounce) can refrigerated pizza dough
⅓ cup tomato paste
1 cup shredded cheese (choose Cheddar, mozzarella, Jack,
    Swiss or a mixture of two or more)

Mom and Dads' Half (all optional)
1 tablespoon red pepper flakes
¼ cup diced onion
1 cup broccoli florets
2 cloves minced garlic
1 teaspoon basil
¼ Parmesan cheese

Preheat oven to pizza-dough directions. Pat dough into a 12 to
14-inch pizza pan. Bake crust for 6-8 minutes (see package
instructions). In a bowl, mix tomato paste and cheese; spread
over dough. On Mom and Dads' half, add optional ingredients.
Return to oven until cheese is melted.

PIZZA DOUGH OPTIONS

If you get tired of the frozen dough at your market (as I do!) get
creative!
* If you have a bread machine, try making dough with that!
Although it takes a while, the process is relatively easy. It's a
perfect option for a Sunday afternoon.

* Many times local pizzerias sell dough that can be used for
pizza and breadsticks.

* Last Christmas, my daughter and I stumbled on a store called
DOWNTOWN DOUGH in nearby Cedarburg. Their shelves were
filled with every pre-made dough imaginable! Breakfast biscuits,
pizza crusts, bread sticks, pies, cookies—you name it, they had
it. We took several bags of cookie dough home for our Christmas
cookies. It was wonderful. We were able to have many cookie
varieties without the cost of a ka-zillion ingredients and each
tasted incredible. They have an internet site at
www.downtowndough.com where you can order your dough to
be delivered. (Don't miss their thousands of cookie cutters
either!)

Grocery List Week Eleven

Produce

- ❑ 2 cloves garlic**
- ❑ ¼ cup diced onion**
- ❑ ½ cup green onions
- ❑ 3 cloves garlic
- ❑ 1 cup broccoli florets**
- ❑ 1 head lettuce*
- ❑ ½ cup shredded carrots*
- ❑ 12 cherry tomatoes*
- ❑ 1 small red onion*

Canned/Boxed Goods

- ❑ ⅓ cup tomato paste
- ❑ ½ taco seasoning packet
- ❑ 1¾ cup bread crumbs
- ❑ 4 cups prepared mashed potatoes
- ❑ 1 cup Italian dressing
- ❑ 2 cans chicken broth
- ❑ 2 cups long grain white rice
- ❑ 1 (15 ounce) can chunky tomato sauce
- ❑ 4 ounces pizza sauce
- ❑ ¾ cup Miracle Whip®

Pantry/Spices

- ❑ Salt
- ❑ Pepper
- ❑ Olive oil
- ❑ Oregano
- ❑ Red pepper flakes**
- ❑ Basil**

Meat

- ❑ 4 boneless chicken breasts
- ❑ 6 chicken breasts
- ❑ 1½ pound ground beef

Dairy

- ❑ 1½ cups Parmesan cheese
- ❑ ⅓ cup milk
- ❑ ½ cup sour cream
- ❑ 3 cans refrigerated pizza crust dough
- ❑ 2½ cups mozzarella cheese
- ❑ 1 cup shredded cheese (your choice)

Frozen

- ❑ 1 cup frozen peas

Other

- ❑ Dressing (or ingredients from page 29-32 to make a dressing)
- ❑ _____
- ❑ _____
- ❑ _____
- ❑ _____
- ❑ _____
- ❑ _____
- ❑ _____
- ❑ _____

*These ingredients are for the Simple Salad (p. 64) side dish.

**These are optional for "Cheese Pizza Please".

Week Twelve Menu

HIP AND HEALTHY STROGANOFF
ROSEMARY BROCCOLI

o

CHEDDAR-Y TURKEY CASSEROLE
CHOICE OF STEAMED VEGGIES

o

MARVELOUS MEATLOAF
POTATO PANCAKES

o

MUSHROOM AND BEEF PASTA
TOMATO BREAD

o

SOY-SKETTI
MARVELOUS MUSHROOM RICE

HIP AND HEALTHY STROGANOFF

1 pound sirloin, cut into strips
2 tablespoons flour
1 cup beef broth
2 cloves garlic, minced
½ teaspoon pepper
4 cups cooked egg noodles
1 (4 ounce) can mushrooms, drained
½ cup nonfat sour cream

Brown meat in skillet over medium heat. In a separate bowl, combine flour, pepper and broth, mix until smooth. Add flour mixture and garlic to pan. Stir over medium-low heat until the meat is done and sauce has thickened. Add mushrooms and sour cream. Heat through. Serve over noodles. Serve with Rosemary Broccoli (page 134). Makes 4 servings.

CLICK FOR SAVINGS

Looking for a way to save money without clipping coupons? Try www.valuepage.com This online site allows you to enter your zip code, choose a supermarket, browse their weekly sales and specials, and click the items you would like to save on. Print your list, hand it to the cashier and you will receive Web Bucks good for any purchase on your next visit.

Note: Even if you consider yourself an Internet Novice, don't be afraid of this site. I promise it is simple and assessable to even the most inexperienced. After all, this is a Rush Hour Book—I promise not to include anything that takes more time than it's worth!

CHEDDAR-Y TURKEY CASSEROLE

1¼ cups instant white rice
2 cups diced turkey
1 (10.5 ounce) can cream of mushroom soup
¾ cup milk
1 cup seasoned stuffing croutons
1 cup shredded Cheddar cheese

Prepare rice according to package directions. Transfer rice to a baking dish. In a medium bowl, mix soup and milk well. Add turkey and croutons to soup mixture and stir well. Spread turkey mixture over rice and top with Cheddar cheese. Bake in a 350-degree oven for 30 minutes. Serve with your choice of steamed veggies (for steaming success secrets, see page 44). Makes 6 servings.

MARVELOUS MEATLOAF

2 eggs
2 (10.5 ounce) cans French onion soup
2 pounds ground round
2 (10.5 ounce) cans cream of mushroom soup
2½ cups crushed butter crackers

Mix all ingredients together except mushroom soup. Shape into 2 equal-size loaves and place in pan. Bake in a 350-degree oven for 40 minutes. Pour mushroom soup over top and bake for another hour. Serve with Potato Pancakes (page 154). Makes 8 servings.

RUSH HOUR TIP

To prevent your meatloaf from cracking, rub a small amount of water on the outside of loaf prior to baking.

POTATO PANCAKES

1 pound potatoes, peeled	2 egg whites
3 tablespoons all-purpose flour	¾ teaspoon salt
2 tablespoons minced scallion	Vegetable oil

Preheat oven to 375 degrees. Shred potatoes and soak in cold water for 30 minutes. Drain and blot dry. In a small bowl, beat egg whites till foamy. In a medium bowl, combine potatoes, egg whites, flour, scallions and salt; mix well. Form into 12 pancakes. In a large nonstick skillet, heat oil over medium heat. Cook pancakes in a single layer in skillet, just until golden on each side, about 2 minutes; transfer to baking sheet. Continue with additional oil and pancakes. Bake 5-8 minutes, until crisp and cooked through. Makes 12 pancakes.

Although meatloaf or potato pancakes aren't technically dough, you are bound to get some helping hands if you let kids squish and mold. You could even get creative by making different meatloaf shapes! Try serving Dad a meatloaf shaped like a remote control, or give Big Brother one shaped like a football (just keep all creative loaves about the same size for even cooking!)

EDIBLE FINGER-PAINTS

Next time you are looking for a way to occupy Junior while cooking, try this quick tip from Penny Stone, author of *365 Quick, Easy and Inexpensive Dinner Menus*. Mix up a box of vanilla instant pudding and divide into several bowls. Lay down a sheet of wax paper. Let your child add a few drops of food coloring to each of the vanilla pudding dishes. Now encourage creativity by letting your child finger-paint on the waxed paper with the pudding mixture. When finished, discard waxed paper, lick fingers and enjoy.

MUSHROOM AND BEEF PASTA

1 pound ground round
½ pound fresh mushrooms, sliced
1 jar prepared marinara sauce
½ teaspoon salt
1 (16 ounce) box of corkscrew pasta
½ cup minced onion
2 cloves garlic, minced
Olive oil

Heat the olive oil over medium heat. Add onions and garlic and sauté for 3 minutes. Add beef and cook until no longer pink. Add mushrooms and cook for an additional 5 minutes. Add marinara sauce, salt and pepper. Bring to a boil while stirring. Reduce heat and simmer for 3 minutes. Serve with Tomato Bread (see page 124). Makes 4 servings.

A NOT-SO-SUBLIMINAL REMINDER

Hey... did you join THE RUSH HOUR CLUB yet? If not, log on to www.rushhourcook.com... you'll get the free DAILY RUSH newsletter with a tip, advice and recipe!

SOY-SKETTI

1 pound spaghetti
¼ cup soy sauce
⅓ cup rice wine vinegar
2 cups chicken, cooked and shredded

Cook spaghetti according to package directions, drain. Heat rice wine vinegar, soy sauce and chicken in a small saucepan over medium-low heat until heated through. Toss with spaghetti and serve. Serve with Marvelous Mushroom Rice (page 156). Makes 6 servings.

MARVELOUS MUSHROOM RICE

2 cups uncooked white rice
1 (10.75 ounce) can condensed cream of mushroom soup
1 cup vegetable broth
⅛ cup water
½ cup fresh mushrooms, sliced or 1 (4 ounce) can mushrooms
1 teaspoon dried oregano
¼ cup butter, melted
¼ teaspoon salt
⅛ teaspoon pepper

Preheat oven to 350 degrees. Stir rice, soup and broth
together in a 2 quart casserole dish. Blend in all other
ingredients. Bake for 35 to 40 minutes or until rice is tender.
Makes 6 servings.

MUCH ADO ABOUT MUSHROOMS

To maximize the life of your mushrooms, do not rinse
before storing. Instead, wrap in a paper bag and store in
refrigerator.

When ready to use, wash quickly in cold water and dry
well. Mushrooms absorb water very quickly, so it's
important to not let them get soaked with water!

Don't buy a load of mushrooms at once. They only retain
their maximum freshness for 2-3 days.

Mushrooms are tricky to cook with since they quickly
change size. As a rule of thumb, you'll need about ¼
pound of mushrooms per serving. One pound of
mushrooms will yield 4-5 cups of sliced raw mushrooms
but when you cook them, they reduce to about 2½ cups.

Grocery List Week Twelve

Produce

- ☐ 2 garlic cloves
- ☐ 1 pound potatoes
- ☐ 1 scallion, optional
- ☐ ½ pound fresh mushrooms
- ☐ 1 onion
- ☐ Choice of veggies for steaming (to serve alongside Cheddar-y Turkey Casserole)
- ☐ 2 pounds broccoli*

Canned/Boxed Goods

- ☐ 2 cups white rice
- ☐ 1 cup beef broth
- ☐ 4 cups egg noodles
- ☐ 2 cans mushrooms
- ☐ 1¼ cups instant white rice
- ☐ 4 cans cream of mushroom soup
- ☐ 2 cans French onion soup
- ☐ 2½ cups crushed butter crackers
- ☐ 1 pound corkscrew pasta
- ☐ 1 pound spaghetti
- ☐ 1 can vegetable broth

Bread

- ☐ 1 cup seasoned croutons

Pantry/Spices

- ☐ Flour
- ☐ Pepper
- ☐ Dried oregano
- ☐ Salt
- ☐ Vegetable oil
- ☐ Olive oil
- ☐ Soy sauce
- ☐ Rice wine vinegar
- ☐ Dried rosemary*
- ☐ Lemon juice*

Meat

- ☐ 1 pound sirloin
- ☐ 2 cups diced turkey
- ☐ 3 pounds ground round
- ☐ 2 cups cooked chicken

Dairy

- ☐ ½ cup sour cream
- ☐ Milk
- ☐ 1 cup shredded Cheddar cheese
- ☐ 4 eggs
- ☐ Butter

*These ingredients are for the Rosemary Broccoli side dish to be served with the Hip and Healthy Stroganoff.

Other

- ☐ _____
- ☐ _____
- ☐ _____
- ☐ _____
- ☐ _____
- ☐ _____
- ☐ _____

NOTES:

Week Thirteen Menu

HAM AND PASTA BAKE

o

CHICKEN CORDON BLUE
TWICE BAKED POTATOES

o

CAJUN CHICKEN
BASIC FETTUCCINI PASTA

o

GRILLED CHEESE PLEASE
FUNKY FRIES

o

GNARLY BARLEY CASSEROLE

HAM AND PASTA BAKE

16 ounces ziti pasta
1½ cups cooked ham, cubed
8 ounces Cheddar cheese
1 can chicken broth
1 (10.5 ounce) can cream of chicken soup
½ cup milk
1 can whole kernel corn

Preheat oven to 350 degrees. Cook pasta according to package directions. Combine pasta, ham, corn and half of cheese in a 9 x 13-inch baking dish coated with cooking spray. Combine broth, soup and milk in bowl. Pour over pasta and mix well. Bake for 30 minutes. Top with remaining cheese and bake just until cheese is melted.

CHICKEN CORDON BLUE

6 skinless, boneless chicken breasts
6 thin slices of low-fat ham
3 tablespoons of nonfat milk
½ cup cornflake crumbs
3 ounces reduced-fat Swiss cheese

Preheat oven to 400 degrees. Cut a slit in each chicken breast and tuck one slice of ham inside. Roll in milk and then dredge in cornflake crumbs. Place in an oil-sprayed baking dish. Bake for 20-25 minutes. Top with cheese and then return to oven until cheese melts. Serve with Twice-Baked Potatoes (page 161). Makes 6 servings.

RUSH HOUR TIP:

Cut meats across grain, when possible, as they will be easier to eat, more tender, and look prettier, too!

TWICE-BAKED POTATOES

6 medium baked potatoes, scrubbed
4 cloves garlic, minced
½ cup milk
½ cup buttermilk
1 teaspoon dried parsley flakes
½ teaspoon salt
½ teaspoon pepper
Paprika for garnish

Preheat oven to 400 degrees. Bake potatoes. Cut ⅓ off of top and scoop out potatoes leaving skins intact. Mash potato innards. Mix rest of ingredients (excluding paprika) with potato innards. Scoop back into potato skins. Bake for 30 minutes. Top with paprika, if desired. Makes 6 servings.

CAJUN CHICKEN

⅓ cup Dijon-style mustard
4 tablespoons Cajun seasoning
6 chicken breasts
½ cup dried bread crumbs

Combine Dijon mustard with 4 tablespoons of Cajun seasoning. Spread over chicken and then dredge in bread crumbs. Cook over medium-high heat in a nonstick skillet for 5-7 minutes on each side or until no longer pink. Serve with Basic Fettuccini Pasta (page 162). Makes 6 servings.

You can use this Cajun recipe with lean pork chops, too!

BASIC FETTUCCINI PASTA

8 ounces fettuccini
⅓ cup grated Parmesan
½ teaspoon salt
2 tablespoons olive oil

8 ounces plain yogurt
3 garlic cloves, minced
½ teaspoon pepper

Cook pasta according to package directions. Combine salt, Parmesan cheese, pepper and yogurt in a small bowl. In a small skillet, sauté garlic in olive oil, being careful not to overcook. Toss pasta, yogurt mixture and garlic all together in a large bowl.

GRILLED CHEESE, PLEASE

12 pieces of toast
Butter
12 pieces of American cheese
Optional: bacon, tomatoes, ham

I think we all know how to make a grilled cheese, so I'll forego the instructions. Kids, of course, love this and parents tend to like it too—especially when you add a bit of bacon and tomato. Never overlook this "classic favorite" as a nice Rush Hour™ dinner solution! Serve with Funky Fries (page 163). Makes 6 sandwiches.

Need to score points with the kids? This menu should do the trick. This is also a great "starter recipe" for kids who are learning to cook. Turn your teen loose and see what happens—maybe you'll get the night off!

FUNKY FRIES

2 egg whites
⅓ cup Italian bread crumbs
2 tablespoons grated Parmesan
1 teaspoon onion salt
½ teaspoon pepper
1 pound baking potatoes

Preheat oven to 350 degrees. Beat egg whites until foamy. Scrub potatoes clean and then slice into circles. Mix bread crumbs, Parmesan, salt and pepper in a small bowl. Dip potatoes in egg-white mixture then dredge in spices. Arrange on cookie sheet in a single layer and bake for 40 minutes. Makes 6 servings.

Serve with loads of ketchup.

GNARLY-BARLEY CASSEROLE

2 teaspoons vegetable oil
1 cup uncooked pearl barley
2 cloves garlic
¼ cup diced onion
2 tablespoons chicken bouillon granules
1 pound cooked chicken breast, cubed
2 cups sliced mushrooms
½ teaspoon basil
2 ounces slivered almonds
3 cups water

Preheat oven to 350 degrees. Heat oil in a large ovenproof pot. Add onions and barley. Cook over medium heat, stirring frequently until onion is browned. Add bouillon and 3 cups water, stir well. Transfer the pot to oven and bake 45 minutes or until barley is cooked. Add chicken, mushrooms and almonds. Stir to combine. Return to oven for an additional 30 minutes, or until casserole is heated through. ***Parents: You may want to bake this in two dishes and add garlic and onion to your portion.***

Grocery List Week Thirteen

Produce

- 2-3 pounds baking potatoes
- 7 cloves garlic
- Optional tomato for grilled cheese
- 2 cups sliced mushrooms
- 1 small onion

Breads

- Your favorite bread for grilled cheese

Canned/Boxed Goods

- 16 ounces ziti pasta
- 1 can cream of chicken soup
- 1 can corn
- 1 can chicken broth
- Cornflakes
- Dijon-style mustard
- 8 ounces fettuccini
- Pearl barley
- Chicken bouillon granules

Pantry/Spices

- Dried parsley flakes
- Pepper
- Salt

Other

- _____
- _____
- _____
- _____
- _____

- Paprika
- Basil
- Cajun seasoning
- Bread crumbs
- Olive oil
- Onion salt
- Italian bread crumbs
- Slivered almonds

Meat

- 1½ cups cooked ham
- 6 skinless, boneless chicken breasts
- 6 thin slices of low-fat ham
- Optional bacon and ham for grilled cheese
- 1 pound cooked chicken breast meat

Dairy

- Milk
- ½ cup buttermilk
- Grated Parmesan cheese
- 2 eggs
- 8 ounces plain yogurt
- Butter
- 12 slices of American cheese
- 3 ounces reduced-fat Swiss cheese
- 8 ounces Cheddar cheese

REALLY GOOD, CREATIVE TACOS

o

CHILI TORTILLA PIE

o

CHICKEN BROTH WITH ANGEL-HAIR PASTA RICOTTA PESTO BREAD

o

LEMON BROILED CHICKEN LYONNAISE POTATOES

o

CHEESE STUFFED MANICOTTI TOMATO BREAD SIMPLE SALAD

REALLY GOOD, CREATIVE TACOS

Filling:
2 tablespoons vegetable oil
2 cups diced potatoes
½ pound ground beef
3 large garlic cloves, minced
½ teaspoon ground cumin
½ teaspoon salt
¼ cup water

Tacos:
8 taco shells and fixings, such as diced
tomatoes, shredded lettuce, cheese and sour
cream

For filling: heat oil in nonstick skillet, add garlic and cook for
2 minutes. Add diced potatoes, cooking until golden brown
but stirring as little as possible. Add ¼ cup water; bring to a
boil. Reduce heat and simmer just until potatoes are tender,
adding cumin and salt. In another pan brown beef. Add ¼ cup
additional water and cook till absorbed. Toss potato mixture
with meat mixture and scoop into tacos. Top with your choice
of toppings. Makes 4 servings.

RUSH HOUR TIP:
PUT YOUR BEST SPUD FORWARD...

Small Potatoes are best for use in salads.

Medium Potatoes work well for just about anything—
mashed, baked, fried, you name it.

Large potatoes are ideal for French fries or the "meal-in-
itself" baked potato.

CHILI-TORTILLA PIE

2 teaspoons corn oil
10 ounces boneless cooked pork
2 cups chopped onions
1 tablespoon mild or hot chili powder
2 garlic cloves, pressed
1½ cups tomato sauce
1 teaspoon dried oregano
8 corn tortillas (6" diameter)
2 ounces shredded Monterey Jack
  cheese

Preheat oven to 375 degrees. In a
nonstick skillet, heat oil; add pork,
onions, chili powder and garlic. Cook over medium-high heat,
stirring occasionally for 5 minutes, until onions are softened.
Add tomato sauce and oregano to pork mixture; bring to a
boil. Reduce heat to low and simmer 5 minutes more. Spray
an 8 x 8-inch baking dish with cooking spray and line with 4
tortillas; top with pork mixture, then remaining tortillas.
Sprinkle with cheese; bake 15 minutes, until lightly browned
and bubbly. Makes 4 servings.

CHICKEN BROTH
WITH ANGEL-HAIR PASTA

5 cups sliced carrots
15 cups low-sodium chicken broth
16 ounces angel-hair pasta
¼ cup Parmesan cheese
Salt and pepper to taste

Steam carrots for 15 minutes or until tender. Cook angel hair
pasta in a 6-quart pot according to package directions, drain
and return to pot. Add broth and carrots. Divide soup among 8
serving bowls and top each portion with Parmesan cheese.
Salt and pepper to taste. Serve with Ricotta Pesto Bread (page
168). Makes 8 servings.

RICOTTA-PESTO BREAD

1 loaf French bread, cut into 12 slices
1 cup part-skim ricotta cheese
6 garlic cloves, minced
3 tablespoons basil flakes
Pepper to taste

Preheat oven to 300 degrees. Place bread slices on a foil-lined baking sheet. Bake for 5 minutes then turn heat up to 400 degrees. Combine remaining ingredients in a blender until well-processed. Spread blended mixture over bread. Bake for 15-20 minutes more or until hot and crispy. Makes 12 servings.

LEMON-BROILED CHICKEN

¼ cup fresh lemon juice
½ teaspoon dried thyme leaves
½ teaspoon dried rosemary leaves
½ teaspoon coarsely ground black pepper
4 boneless, skinless chicken breasts
*Serve with steamed broccoli

Combine lemon juice, thyme, rosemary and pepper in a small bowl. Rub half of the lemon mixture on chicken. Place chicken beneath heated broiler, turning once after 5 minutes or until browned and cooked through. Remove chicken, drizzle with rest of lemon mixture and serve. Serve with Lyonnaise Potatoes (page 169). Makes 4 servings.

*Steamed broccoli is a great choice as an accompaniment. You may also wish to double the lemon mixture and drizzle over the broccoli as well. For steaming instructions, see STEAMING SUCCESS on page 44.

LYONNAISE POTATOES

2 tablespoons oil
1½ pounds boiled potatoes, peeled and sliced ¼-inch thick
¼ teaspoon dried marjoram leaves
⅛ teaspoon white pepper
1 cup thinly sliced onions
2 garlic cloves, slivered
¼ cup chicken broth

Heat 1 tablespoon olive oil in a skillet. Add potatoes and sprinkle with salt, marjoram and pepper. Cook over medium heat, about 10 minutes, turning occasionally. While potatoes are cooking, heat the other tablespoon of oil in a separate skillet. Add onions. Cook 3-4 minutes. Lower heat, add garlic and cook 2 minutes. Add broth; cook 5-7 minutes more, until garlic and onions are soft. Transfer onions to pan with potatoes and toss together. Makes 4 servings.

You won't win over kids who hate onions with this potato dish! Reserve some potatoes prior to adding onions!

YOU DON'T HAVE TO CRY ABOUT IT: CURES FOR ONION EYES

I confess, I have not tried all of these, but I rounded them up in my research for "onion eyes." Give them a whirl and let me know what works best for you! (See how to contact me at the back of this book.)

* Place onions in freezer for 20 minutes prior to cutting
* Cut onions under cold running water
* My favorite (which I have done)—Go ahead and cry while cutting a ton of onions at one time. Then freeze in ½ cup increments in airtight freezer containers. Pull out as needed. Frozen onions will keep for 2 months.
* My second favorite—Have any child over 12 cut them as a punishment for misbehavior.
* Ask for a food processor for Christmas! You can also find a much less expensive solution at most cookware stores in the form of small gadgets that hand dice onions, mushrooms and more.

CHEESE-STUFFED MANICOTTI

2 teaspoons olive oil
3 cups tomato sauce
½ teaspoon black pepper
6 ounces mozzarella cheese
1 egg, lightly beaten
12 cooked manicotti shells

5 garlic cloves, crushed
1 tablespoon Italian seasoning
1½ cups ricotta cheese
¾ cup grated Parmesan cheese

Preheat oven to 350 degrees. Sauté garlic in oil over medium heat for 2 minutes. Add tomato sauce, Italian seasoning and pepper; mix well. Reduce heat to low; simmer, covered, stirring occasionally for 15 minutes. In a medium bowl, combine cheeses, egg and parsley. Fill each manicotti shell with cheese mixture. Arrange shells in 9 x 13-inchbaking dish coated with cooking spray. Pour sauce over stuffed shells. Bake 30-40 minutes. Makes 6 servings. Tomato Bread (page 124) and Simple Salad (page 64) compliment this meal nicely.

RUSH HOUR TIP

Make extra manicotti and freeze! Do not bake. Wrap each cheese-stuffed manicotti carefully in foil and store foil-wrapped manicotti in an air-tight freezer bag. To serve, remove manicotti the night before using and let thaw in refrigerator. Carefully unwrap manicotti and place in baking dish. Pour sauce over top and bake in a 350-degree oven for 1 hour or until heated through. These keep well for about 2 months in the freezer. Make sure to label and date the packages when you freeze them!

Grocery List Week Fourteen

Produce
- 18 cloves garlic
- 2½ pounds potatoes
- 3 tomatoes
- Shredded lettuce
- 4 large onions
- 1 large package carrots
- 2 lemons
- Fresh broccoli
- 1 head lettuce*
- 1 small red onion*
- ½ cup shredded carrots*
- 12 cherry tomatoes*

Breads
- 2 loaves French bread

Canned/Boxed Goods
- 8 taco shells
- 3 cups tomato sauce
- 16 ounces angel hair pasta
- 15¼ cups low-sodium chicken broth
- 12 manicotti shells
- Lemon juice

Pantry/Spices
- Ground cumin
- Salt
- Corn oil
- Vegetable oil
- Chili powder
- Oregano
- White pepper
- Pepper
- Basil flakes
- Thyme
- Rosemary
- Olive oil
- Italian seasoning
- Marjoram leaves, dried

Meat
- ½ pound ground beef
- 10 ounces boneless, cooked pork or skinless turkey
- 4 boneless, skinless chicken breasts

Dairy
- Cheddar cheese
- Sour cream
- 2 ounces shredded Monterey Jack cheese
- 8 corn tortillas
- Parmesan cheese
- 2½ cups part-skim ricotta cheese
- 6 ounces mozzarella cheese
- 1 egg
- Butter

Other
- Dressing (or add ingredients from dressing of choice on pages 29-32)*
- _____
- _____
- _____

❑ _____
❑ _____
❑ _____
❑ _____
❑ _____

*These ingredients are for the Simple Salad side dish to be served with the Cheese-Stuffed Manicotti

NOTES:

_____
_____
_____
_____
_____
_____
_____
_____
_____
_____
_____
_____
_____
_____
_____
_____
_____

Week Fifteen Menu

BEEF ENCHILADA CASSEROLE

○

CAJUN FLANK STEAK
TWICE-AS-NICE VEGGIE RICE

○

SHREDDED BEEF SANDWICHES
AWESOME APPLE COBBLER

○

NOODLE BAKE
PARMESAN GARLIC TOASTS

○

TUSCAN STYLE PORK ROAST WITH
CINNAMON BAKED APPLES

BEEF ENCHILADA CASSEROLE

2 cups canned red chili sauce
2 tablespoons all-purpose flour
4 cups tomato puree
1 teaspoon chili powder
1 pound ground beef
½ cup diced onion
12 (6-inch) corn tortillas, quartered
4 ounces Cheddar cheese, shredded

Preheat oven to 350 degrees. Mix flour and chili sauce over medium-low heat. Once heated through add tomato puree and chili powder. Bring to a boil and stir constantly until mixture thickens slightly. Remove from heat. Brown beef and onions in a nonstick skillet coated with cooking spray, over medium heat. In a 9 x 13-inch casserole dish spread ½ cup of sauce then a layer of corn tortillas. Top with ⅓ of meat mixture and ⅓ of cheese. Repeat layers. Bake covered, for 30 minutes, then uncovered for an additional 5 minutes. Makes 6 servings.

Most of the Mexican dishes included in this book offer a great starting point for soft tacos! If your kids prefer "plainer" foods, reserve a tortilla along with some meat and cheese, before completing the "adult recipe".

CAJUN FLANK STEAK

2 tablespoons Worcestershire sauce, divided
2 teaspoons hot pepper sauce
2 garlic cloves, minced
1 teaspoon dried thyme
1 pound flank steak, scored on both sides
2 tablespoons low-sodium beef broth

In a small bowl, combine 1 tablespoon of the Worcestershire sauce, 1 teaspoon of the hot pepper sauce, garlic and thyme; rub steak with mixture. Let stand 10 minutes. Place steak on preheated broiler rack; broil for 3-5 minutes on each side or until done. Combine remaining Worcestershire sauce and hot pepper sauce with broth. Slice steak into thin pieces. Arrange steak on platter and top with sauce. Serve with Twice as Nice Veggie Rice (page 123). Makes 4 servings.

SHREDDED BEEF SANDWICHES

These sandwiches are definitely a meal in themselves! For that reason, I did not include a side dish. Just in case you are still hungry, I've included a great apple cobbler recipe on the following page to finish off the meal!

2 sticks butter
1 beef roast (2-3 pounds)
Water
2 tablespoons white wine vinegar
2 tablespoons Worcestershire sauce
2 tablespoons barbecue sauce
French bread

Melt 1 stick of butter in a Dutch oven. Brown roast on all sides. Add ½ cup water and second stick of butter to roast; cover and simmer for 4 hours adding more water as needed. Remove beef and shred with fork. Return to pot and mix in remaining ingredients. Simmer for 20 minutes and then serve open faced on French bread. Serve with Awesome Apple Cobbler (page 176). Makes 8-10 servings.

AWESOME APPLE COBBLER

1 cup buttermilk
¾ cup buttermilk baking mix
2 tablespoons granulated sugar, divided
½ teaspoon ground cardamom
4 Granny Smith apples, cored, pared and thinly sliced
2 tablespoons fresh lemon juice

Preheat oven to 350 degrees. Spray a 1-quart baking dish with cooking spray. In a small bowl, combine buttermilk, baking mix, 1 tablespoon of the sugar and the cardamom; stir until smooth. Set aside. In a medium saucepan, combine apples, the remaining 1 tablespoon sugar and the lemon juice; bring to a boil. Reduce heat to low; cook, stirring constantly, 5 minutes or until fruit becomes soft. Transfer apple mixture to baking dish. Drop buttermilk mixture by the spoonful over fruit. Bake for 20 minutes or until cooked through and bubbly. Makes 4 servings.

ADD SOME SPICE TO YOUR LIFE!

More for fun than a Freudian study, here are what some popular herbs represent:

Basil	Love (or hate)
Bay	Victory
Lavender	Acknowledgement
Fennel	Praise
Caraway	Retention
Marjoram	Happiness
Mints	Wisdom
Rosemary	Remembrance
Sage	Long Life
Thyme	Bravery

So the next time you are feeling under the weather, stock up on the marjoram!

NOODLE BAKE

1 teaspoon olive oil	1 cup minced onions
1 teaspoon dried oregano	¼ cup grated Parmesan
1⅓ cups fat-free ricotta cheese	¼ teaspoon salt
¼ teaspoon ground black pepper	6 ounces egg noodles
2 cups chopped mushrooms	1½ cups tomato sauce

Preheat oven to 400 degrees. Prepare noodles according to package directions. Spray an 8-inch square baking pan with nonstick cooking spray. In a medium skillet, heat oil; add onions. Cook over medium-high heat, stirring frequently, 3-4 minutes or until golden brown. Remove skillet from heat; stir in oregano. Transfer half of onion mixture to small bowl; add ricotta cheese, salt and black pepper, stir well. Set aside. To onion mixture remaining in skillet, add mushrooms and tomato sauce. Bring to a boil over medium-high heat. Reduce heat. Simmer until vegetables are tender. Place noodles in baking pan; top with ricotta cheese mixture, then vegetable mixture. Sprinkle with Parmesan cheese and bake for 20 minutes or until heated through. Serve with Parmesan-Garlic Toasts (below). Makes 4 servings.

Most kids love these noodle bake dishes! You can hide a lot of herbs, spices and finely chopped vegetables when you blend them with meat, cheese and pasta!

PARMESAN-GARLIC TOASTS

6 garlic cloves, chopped
2 teaspoons olive oil
½ loaf French bread, cut into 12 thin slices
½ cup grated Parmesan cheese

Preheat oven to 400 degrees. Line a baking sheet with foil. In a small saucepan, combine ½ cup water, garlic and oil. Bring to a boil. Reduce heat to low and simmer 10 minutes or until thickened and smooth. Spread mixture on bread slices then place on baking sheet. Sprinkle evenly with Parmesan cheese. Bake 10 minutes or until crisp.

TUSCAN-STYLE PORK ROAST

2-3 pound pork loin (on the bone)	4 garlic cloves, halved
2 tablespoons olive oil	1 tablespoon rosemary
½ teaspoon pepper	½ teaspoon salt
½ cup dry white wine	

Make small slits in the roast and insert slivers of garlic. In a small bowl mix oil, rosemary, pepper and salt. Rub roast with oil mixture. Place roast in a shallow roasting pan and pour wine over roast. Place roast in a 350-degree oven and baste occasionally with wine and pan juices, until cooked through and browned, about 1½ hours. (Always use a meat thermometer to check for doneness!) Slice and serve. Serve with Cinnamon Baked Apples (page 179). Makes 8-12 servings.

MEAT PRIMER

Here is a quick overview of different meats available at your local market.

Rib: Somewhat tender. Examples include rib-eye steak for grilling and standing rib roast.

Short Loin: The most tender and thus most expensive (this includes filet mignon, Porterhouse, T-bone, top-loin)

Sirloin: Tender, but not like the short loin. Sirloin steak and sirloin tips are two forms of this, slice thin when serving.

Round: Not too tender. Good choice for lower-cost crock pot recipes or other recipes where meat cooks for a long time and becomes tender through cooking.

Brisket and Shank: Like the above, these meats need to be cooked in recipes where they are tenderized by extended cooking. Stew meat is an example.

CINNAMON BAKED APPLES

4 small apples   4 teaspoons light brown sugar
Cinnamon

Preheat oven to 450 degrees. Core apples and place in baking pan. Sprinkle with brown sugar and cinnamon; bake, covered, 15 minutes or until tender but not mushy.

ANOTHER REASON TO EAT APPLES

Not only may an apple a day keep the doctor away but researchers at Yale University have discovered that the scent of apples can help people relax and reduce stress!

Produce

- ❑ 3 heads garlic
- ❑ 2 large onions
- ❑ 2 cups mushrooms
- ❑ 4 Granny Smith apples
- ❑ 4 cooking apples
- ❑ 2 cups bean sprouts*
- ❑ 1 cup shredded carrots*
- ❑ Ginger root*
- ❑ 1½ cup sliced mushrooms*
- ❑ 1 bunch green onions*

Breads

- ❑ 2 loaves French bread

Canned/Boxed Goods

- ❑ 2 cups canned red chili sauce
- ❑ 4 cups tomato puree
- ❑ Beef broth
- ❑ Barbecue sauce
- ❑ Worcestershire sauce
- ❑ Hot pepper sauce
- ❑ 1 can tomato sauce
- ❑ Egg noodles
- ❑ Buttermilk baking mix
- ❑ Lemon juice
- ❑ 3 cups long-grain white rice*

Pantry/Spices

- ❑ Flour
- ❑ Chili powder
- ❑ Thyme
- ❑ White wine vinegar
- ❑ Olive oil
- ❑ Oregano
- ❑ Pepper
- ❑ Salt
- ❑ ½ cup dry white wine
- ❑ Rosemary
- ❑ Sugar
- ❑ Cardamom
- ❑ Cinnamon
- ❑ Brown sugar
- ❑ Soy sauce*

Meat

- ❑ 2-3 pound pork loin (on the bone)
- ❑ 1 pound ground beef
- ❑ 1 pound flank steak
- ❑ 2-3 pound beef roast

Dairy

- ❑ 12 six-inch corn tortillas
- ❑ 4 ounces shredded sharp cheddar cheese
- ❑ 2 sticks butter
- ❑ 1⅓ cups fat-free ricotta cheese
- ❑ Grated Parmesan cheese
- ❑ 1 cup buttermilk

Frozen

- ❑ 1 cup frozen peas*

Other

- ❑ _____
- ❑ _____
- ❑ _____
- ❑ _____
- ❑ _____
- ❑ _____

☐ _____
☐ _____
☐ _____
☐ _____
☐ _____
☐ _____
☐ _____
☐ _____
☐ _____
☐ _____

☐ _____
☐ _____

*These items are for the Twice as Nice Veggie Rice (pg. 123) which is served with the Cajun Flank Steak.

NOTES:

_____

_____

_____

_____

_____

_____

_____

_____

_____

_____

_____

_____

_____

_____

_____

_____

_____

NOTES:

Week Sixteen Menu

SPEEDY CHICKEN FAJITAS
TWICE AS NICE VEGGIE RICE

○

MARINATED FLANK STEAK
BAKED POTATO BONANZA

○

CHICKEN-RICOTTA PASTA BAKE
CORN ON THE COB

○

CHICKEN AND CHEESE ENCHILADAS
FIESTA CORN

○

GROUND BEEF PITA PIZZA
CHOICE OF STEAMED VEGGIES

SPEEDY CHICKEN FAJITAS

1 pound prepared chicken strips (like Louis Rich™)
2 tablespoons fresh lime juice
3 garlic cloves, pressed
8 flour tortillas
Toppings of choice onion, cheese, sour cream, lettuce, etc.

Toss chicken with lime juice and garlic. Warm in microwave until heated through. Wrap tortillas in foil and heat in oven for 3-5 minutes. Serve mixture with tortillas and condiments. Serve with Twice-As-Nice Veggie Rice (page 123). Makes 4 servings.

MARINATED FLANK STEAK

1 pound flank steak
2 tablespoons balsamic vinegar
2 teaspoons reduced-sodium soy sauce
2 teaspoons vegetable oil
1 teaspoon freshly ground black pepper

Make 8 diagonal, criss-crossing slashes about ⅛-inch deep along top of steak. In gallon-size sealable plastic bag, combine vinegar, soy sauce, oil, pepper and then add steak. Seal and turn to coat steak thoroughly. Let marinate 15 minutes, turning occasionally. Preheat broiler. Drain marinade into small saucepan; bring to a boil. Remove from heat; set aside and keep warm. Place steak on rack in broiler pan; broil 4 inches from heat 3-5 minutes on each side until browned and done to desired taste. Slice steak on the diagonal and drizzle with marinade. Serve with Baked Potato Bonanza (page 116). Makes 4 servings.

CHICKEN-RICOTTA PASTA BAKE

6 ounces penne pasta
1 cup sun-dried tomatoes, chopped and re-hydrated (to re-
  hydrate, follow package directions)
1 onion, thinly sliced and separated into rings
2 garlic cloves, minced
2 cups diced tomatoes
1½ cups ricotta cheese
1 teaspoon dried basil leaves
½ pound cooked, shredded chicken
4½ ounces shredded mozzarella cheese
⅛ teaspoon salt

Preheat oven to 350 degrees. Cook pasta according to package
directions. Drain. Cook onion in oil over medium-heat for 3-5
minutes or until tender. Add diced tomatoes and re-hydrated
sun-dried tomatoes. Warm. Reduce heat to low and simmer
10-15 minutes, until liquid is reduced and sauce is thickened.
Add pasta and stir in gently. Set aside. Spray a 9 x 13-inch
casserole dish with nonstick cooking spray. In a medium bowl,
combine ricotta cheese, salt and basil. Layer half of pasta in
bottom of pan. Spread ricotta mixture over pasta and sprinkle
with chicken. Top with remaining pasta mixture; sprinkle with
mozzarella cheese. Bake 25-30 minutes or until heated
through. Serve with Corn on the Cob (page 83). Makes 6
servings.

CHICKEN AND CHEESE ENCHILADAS

¾ cup nonfat sour cream
½ cup thinly sliced scallions
¼ cup minced fresh cilantro
½ teaspoon ground cumin
10 ounces skinless boneless chicken breasts, cut into strips
½ teaspoon salt
2 teaspoons vegetable oil
2 garlic cloves, minced
4 (6-inch) flour tortillas
3 ounces Cheddar cheese, grated
½ cup salsa, you choose the heat
½ cup chopped tomato

Preheat oven to 350 degrees. In a small bowl, combine sour cream, scallions, minced cilantro and cumin; set aside. Sprinkle chicken with salt. Heat oil in a large nonstick skillet; add chicken and garlic. Cook over medium-high heat, stirring frequently, until chicken is cooked through (4-8 minutes). To make enchiladas, spread chicken mixture down each tortilla's center. Fold sides of tortilla over filling and place seam-side-down into a 9 x 13-inch baking pan coated with nonstick cooking spray. Sprinkle cheese over top. Cover. Bake enchiladas 25 minutes, until filling is hot and cheese is melted. Transfer enchiladas to serving plates and top with salsa and freshly cut tomato. Serve with Fiesta Corn (page 187). Makes 4 servings.

FIESTA CORN

2 large cans of niblet corn
1 green bell pepper, diced
1 red bell pepper, diced
½ cup onion, diced
Freshly ground black pepper
1 tablespoon butter

Warm butter in saucepan. Add onions and cook 2-3 minutes or until tender and transparent. Add green and red peppers and cook two minutes more. Add corn and mix well. Cook until heated through. Add freshly ground black pepper prior to serving. Makes 6-8 servings.

RUSH HOUR TIP

Keep a jar of minced garlic on hand to avoid having to mince your own.

GROUND BEEF PITA PIZZA

4 pita breads, split in half
4 ounces lean ground beef
2 garlic cloves, minced
1 cup tomato sauce
1 teaspoon dried oregano leaves
5 ounces mozzarella cheese, grated

Preheat oven to 425 degrees. Place pita rounds on a nonstick baking sheet and bake 5-10 minutes or until toasted. Remove pitas from oven, but leave oven on. Meanwhile add beef and garlic to a skillet coated with cooking spray. Cook meat until browned. Remove from heat. Spread each pita with 2 tablespoons tomato sauce. Top sauce with oregano, then cheese, then meat. Bake 5 minutes, until sauce is bubbling and cheese is melted. Serve with choice of steamed vegetables. For steaming tips see page 44. Makes 8 servings.

Grocery List Week Sixteen

Produce
- 9 cloves garlic
- 1 green bell pepper
- 1 red bell pepper
- 3 onions
- 3 cups diced tomatoes
- ½ cup scallions
- Veggies of your choice to serve steamed with Ground Beef Pita Pizza
- 6 cobs of corn
- 6 baking potatoes
- 2 cups bean sprouts*
- 1 cup shredded carrots*
- Ginger root*
- 1½ cups sliced mushrooms*
- 1 bunch green onions*
- Fresh cilantro

Breads
- 4 pita breads

Canned/Boxed Goods
- Lime juice
- Penne pasta
- 8 ounces sun-dried tomatoes
- ½ cup salsa
- 2 cans niblet corn
- 1 cup tomato sauce
- 3 cups long-grain white rice*

Pantry/Spices
- Balsamic vinegar
- Soy sauce*
- Vegetable oil
- Salt
- Pepper
- Basil
- Cumin
- Dried oregano
- Olive oil

Meat
- 1 pound prepared chicken strips
- 1 pound flank steak
- ½ pound cooked chicken
- 10 ounces boneless chicken breasts
- 4 ounces ground beef

Dairy
- 12 flour tortillas
- Shredded cheese for Fajitas
- 1½ cup ricotta cheese
- 10 ounces mozzarella cheese
- Sour cream
- 3 ounces Cheddar cheese
- Butter

Frozen
- 1 cup frozen peas*

Other
- Toppings of choice for Baked Potato Bonanza (see page 116) served with Marinated Flank Steak.

- ❏ Topping of choice for Speedy Chicken Fajitas (page 184).
- ❏ _____
- ❏ _____
- ❏ _____
- ❏ _____
- ❏ _____
- ❏ _____

- ❏ _____
- ❏ _____

*These ingredients are for the Twice as Nice Veggies Rice (pg. 123) which is served with the Speedy Chicken Fajitas.

NOTES:

_____

_____

_____

_____

_____

_____

_____

_____

_____

_____

_____

_____

_____

_____

_____

NOTES:

Week Seventeen Menu

TACO REVIVAL
CRAZY CORN CASSEROLE

○

LINGUINI WITH HERB BUTTER
TOMATO BREAD

○

LEMON ANGEL-HAIR PASTA
PARMESAN-GARLIC TOASTS

○

HAMBURGER CLUBS
FUNKY FRIES

○

BASIL CHICKEN WITH WILD RICE
ROSEMARY BROCCOLI

TACO REVIVAL

This recipe is based on chilaquiles, a Mexican mainstay. Once you taste it, you'll know why!

1 cup thinly sliced onions, separated into rings
6 (6-inch) corn tortillas, cut into strips
½ pound skinless boneless chicken breasts, cooked and shredded
2 tomatoes, diced
1 cup salsa, you choose the heat
¾ cup low-sodium chicken broth
3 ounces Cheddar cheese, grated

Preheat oven to 350 degrees. Cook onions for 2-3 minutes over medium-high heat in a sprayed nonstick skillet. Spray a 9 x 13-inchbaking pan with nonstick cooking spray. Place half the tortilla strips into pan, covering the bottom. Top tortillas with half the chicken, half the tomatoes, half the cooked onions and half the salsa; repeat layers. Pour broth over mixture; bake, covered, 25-30 minutes. Sprinkle cheese on top and bake, uncovered, for 10 minutes more or until cheese is melted. Serve with Crazy Corn Casserole (below). Makes 6 servings.

You can use beef with this recipe, too. For kids who like a simpler meal, reserve meat, cheese and a soft tortilla. Roll and serve!

CRAZY CORN CASSEROLE

2 cans Mexican-style corn
1 cup milk
1 cup shredded Cheddar cheese

4 eggs
4 tablespoons flour
Salt and pepper to taste

Preheat oven to 350 degrees. Mix flour, salt and pepper. Slowly add milk, then eggs, corn and cheese. Mix gently till combined. Transfer mixture to a 2- quart baking dish coated with cooking spray and bake for 1 hour. Makes 6 servings.

LINGUINE WITH HERB BUTTER

⅓ cup butter
6 tablespoons minced fresh parsley
3 tablespoons minced fresh basil
3 tablespoons minced fresh thyme leaves
3 tablespoons minced fresh oregano
5 garlic cloves, crushed
¼ teaspoon salt
⅛ teaspoon pepper
12 ounces linguine

Cook the linguine according to package directions. While linguine is cooking, melt butter in a skillet over medium heat. Add the parsley, basil, thyme, oregano, garlic, salt and pepper. Reduce the heat to low and cook 30 seconds, until the herbs wilt. Discard garlic. Toss herb mixture and linguine together. Serve with Tomato Bread (page 124). Makes 6 servings.

RUSH HOUR TIP

Plenty of boiling water is the key to perfect pasta. Make sure that you have enough water to let noodles circulate freely. A 6-quart pot should do the trick!

LEMON ANGEL-HAIR PASTA

6 ounces angel-hair pasta
2 teaspoons olive oil
4 garlic cloves
¼ cup minced fresh parsley
2 tablespoons fresh lemon juice
¼ teaspoon salt
⅛ teaspoon pepper

Cook angel hair in boiling water for 3 minutes. Drain. Meanwhile, in medium skillet cook garlic in oil. Crush garlic with fork and cook 2-3 minutes or until tender. Add cooked angel hair, parsley, lemon juice, pepper and salt; toss to coat. Serve sprinkled with pepper. Serve with Parmesan Garlic Toasts (page 177). Makes 4 servings.

HAMBURGER CLUB

½ pound ground beef
12 bread slices
4 tablespoons fat-free Miracle Whip®
8 iceberg lettuce leaves
8 strips low-fat turkey bacon
2 tomatoes, sliced
Salt and pepper taste

Preheat broiler. Spray broiler pan with cooking spray. Form beef into four (4-inch) patties. Broil 4 inches from heat, turning once after 5 minutes and continue until cooked through. Cook bacon according to package directions. Toast bread and then spread each slice with Miracle Whip®. Assemble sandwiches as follows: 1 toast slice, spread-side up topped with 1 lettuce leaf, 2 strips bacon, another toast slice, one slice lettuce, burger, sliced tomatoes, salt and pepper. Top with another toast slice, spread-side down. Serve with Funky Fries (page 163). Makes 4 servings.

BASIL CHICKEN WITH WILD RICE

3 (10.75 ounce) cans cream of mushroom soup
1 (4 ounce) can sliced mushrooms, drained
1 (6 ounce) box wild rice mix
½ cup uncooked white rice (not instant)
½ cup butter, melted
8 skinless, boneless chicken breasts
1 teaspoon dried basil (or 1 tablespoon fresh)
Salt and pepper to taste

Preheat oven to 275 degrees. Combine soup, mushrooms, wild rice with seasoning packet and white rice. Spread into a 3-quart baking dish that has been coated with cooking spray. Rinse chicken and pat dry. Dip chicken into melted butter and lay atop mixture. Drizzle remaining butter on top of casserole. Sprinkle with salt and pepper. Cook for two hours. Serve with Rosemary Broccoli (see page 134). Makes 8 servings.

Grocery List Week Seventeen

Produce
- Onion
- 6 tomatoes
- Fresh parsley
- Fresh basil
- Fresh thyme
- Fresh oregano
- 2 heads garlic
- 1 head iceberg lettuce
- 2 pounds broccoli*

Breads
- 12 slices bread
- French bread**
- 4 pita breads

Canned/Boxed Goods
- Salsa
- 1 can chicken broth
- 2 cans Mexican-style corn
- 12 ounces linguine
- 6 ounces angel hair
- Fresh lemon juice
- 4 tablespoons Miracle Whip™
- 3 cans cream of mushroom soup
- 1 (4 ounce) can sliced mushrooms
- 1 (6 ounce) box wild rice mix
- ½ cup long grain rice

Pantry/Spices
- Flour
- Oregano
- Salt
- Pepper
- Olive oil
- Basil
- Rosemary*
- Lemon juice*

Meat
- ½ pound boneless chicken breasts
- ½ pound ground beef
- 8 skinless, boneless chicken breasts
- 8 strips turkey bacon

Dairy
- 6 corn tortillas
- 11 ounces Cheddar cheese
- Milk
- 4 eggs
- Butter
- Parmesan cheese**

Other

*These ingredients are for the Rosemary Broccoli side dish (p. 134).

**These ingredients are for Parmesan Garlic Toast (p. 177) and/or Tomato Bread (p. 124).

- _____
- _____
- _____
- _____
- _____
- _____

NOTES:

Week Eighteen Menu

BROCCOLI BAKE
EASY PASTA TOSS

o

ROAST BEEF AND GRAVY
POTATO SQUARES

o

PIZZA BURGERS
POTATO WEDGES

o

TOSS-IT-TOGETHER LASAGNA
CHOOSE-A-WAY BREADSTICKS

o

SPAGHETTI PIE
SIMPLE SALAD

BROCCOLI BAKE

3 cups broccoli, rinsed and cut into 1-inch pieces
8 ounces stuffing (such as Stove-Top®)
1 can cream-style corn
1 egg
1 stick butter, melted
1 onion, diced

Preheat oven to 350 degrees. Prepare stuffing according to package directions. Mix all ingredients and place in a 9 x 13-inch casserole dish. Bake for one hour. Serve with Easy Pasta Toss (page 61). Makes 6 servings.

ROAST BEEF & GRAVY

1 (3 pound) beef chuck roast
¼ cup beef broth
¼ cup red wine
2 cans cream of mushroom soup
1 package onion soup mix

Cut roast in half and toss in a crock pot. Mix other ingredients together, pour over roast. Cover and cook on low setting 8-9 hours or high setting for 4½-5 hours. Serve with Potato Squares (page 199). Makes 8-12 servings.

POTATO SQUARES

3 cups cooked mashed potatoes (instant is fine)
2 tablespoons flour
1 egg
1 teaspoon salt
½ teaspoon pepper
½ cup Swiss cheese, shredded
6 slices bacon, crumbled
½ cup sour cream

Preheat oven to 350 degrees. Mix potatoes, flour, salt and pepper and spread into a 9 x 9-inch greased baking dish. Mix sour cream and egg and spread over potato layer. Top with cheese, then bacon. Bake for 30 minutes or until set. Cut into six squares. Makes 6 servings.

HOW TO BECOME A CERTIFIED POTATO-HEAD

Is your child in love with the potato? Now he or she can join the "Spuddy Buddy Club". They can enjoy a free membership and download fun activities through Spuddy's Fan Club. To become a member log on to: www.idahopotato.com and click on Spuddy Buddy.

PIZZA BURGERS

3 pounds ground round
1 small onion, chopped fine
¼ pound Cheddar cheese, shredded
½ pound mozzarella cheese, shredded
1 can pizza sauce
2 tablespoons chili powder
2 teaspoons salt
2 tablespoons dry mustard

Combine all ingredients and form into patties. Bake in a 350-degree oven for 30 minutes or fry in a pan, turning once, until done. This makes a lot of burgers—that's all the better reason to freeze some for quick snacks or dinners! Serve with Funky Fries (page 163). Makes a motherload!

RUSH HOUR TIP:

I strongly promote cooking a bit extra when you can! Why go through all the hassle twice, when you could just do it once and have the same great-tasting results? Once you start stashing favorites away remember to look at your upcoming plans for the week. Note any nights you will need "freezer meals". Transfer the meals you need to the refrigerator to thaw. See the Art of Bulk Cooking on page 37 for more ideas.

TOSS-IT-TOGETHER LASAGNA

1 pound ground round
6 ounces spiral noodles
1 cup cottage cheese
2½ cups shredded mozzarella cheese
2 cups store-bought spaghetti sauce

Preheat oven to 350 degrees. Brown beef. Stir in spaghetti
sauce and simmer for 10 minutes. Pour ½ of mixture into a 9
x 13-inch baking dish. Prepare noodles according to package
directions and drain. Pour ½ of noodles over beef sauce. Mix
cottage and mozzarella cheeses and place ½ of cheese mixture
over noodles. Repeat an additional set of layers. Bake for 30
minutes. Serve with Choose-A-Way Breadsticks (page 202).
Makes 6 servings.

NOTE: This is another great dish that freezes easily! Transfer
to air-tight containers before baking. To finish, thaw and bake
for 45 minutes or until heated through.

POTATO RESUSCITATION 101

If you find yourself with lumpy, gummy or pasty
potatoes—never fear. As a Rush Hour Cook Specialist one
of my many talents is reincarnating what looks to be
ruined food. Simply stir in three tablespoons of minced
onion and a beaten egg yolk. Form into ½-inch thick patty
shapes, 3 inches crosswise. Cook in a tad of butter over
medium-high heat until nicely browned for perfect potato
patties!

CHOOSE-A-WAY BREAD STICKS

Each refrigerated can of breadstick dough makes 8 breadsticks

7 Toppings to Try:

Bruchetta: Chopped tomatoes, chopped fresh parsley and olive oil

Greek: Chopped black or Kalamata olives, feta cheese, and basil

Three cheese: Cheddar, Parmesan and mozzarella

Ham and cheese: Thinly sliced deli ham, Swiss cheese and Dijon-style mustard

Pizza: Pepperoni, mozzarella cheese and pizza sauce

Herbed: Fresh chopped oregano, basil and cilantro (or dried)

Garlic bread: Melted butter and minced garlic (1 teaspoon for every 3 tablespoons butter or you will smell very nice the next day!)

Here's what to do: Preheat oven according to the package directions on the refrigerated breadsticks. Separate dough into strips. Brush dough with your choice of olive oil, melted butter or Italian dressing. Place toppings on top of dough and twist. Brush again with oil or butter. Bake according to directions on package.

Italian food ranks as the most popular ethnic food in America.
Source: National Restaurant Association.

SPAGHETTI PIE

12 ounces spaghetti noodles
1 pound ground round
1 egg
8 ounces mozzarella cheese, grated
1 (32 ounce) jar prepared spaghetti sauce (like Ragu®)
½ cup grated Parmesan cheese
½ teaspoon garlic powder

Cook noodles according to package directions and drain. Mix egg, Parmesan cheese and garlic powder in a small bowl. Toss noodles with egg mixture and press into a 9 x 13-inch, spray-coated baking dish. Brown meat and drain. Mix sauce and meat together and pour over spaghetti. Top with mozzarella cheese. Bake in a 350-degree oven for 35-40 minutes. Serve with Simple Salad (page 64). Makes 6 servings.

Grocery List Week Eighteen

Produce
- ☐ 3 cups broccoli
- ☐ 2 onions
- ☐ 1 pound baking potatoes
- ☐ 1 head lettuce*
- ☐ 12 cherry tomatoes*
- ☐ ½ cup shredded carrot*
- ☐ 1 small red onion*

Breads
- ☐ 1-2 cans refrigerated bread stick dough and choice of toppings for Choose-A-Way Breadsticks (p. 202)

Canned/Boxed Goods
- ☐ 8 ounces stuffing mix
- ☐ 1 can cream-style corn
- ☐ 3 cups prepared mashed potatoes
- ☐ ¼ cup beef broth
- ☐ ¼ cup red wine
- ☐ 2 cans cream of mushroom soup
- ☐ 1 package onion soup mix
- ☐ 1 can pizza sauce
- ☐ 6 ounces spiral noodles
- ☐ 48 ounces store bought spaghetti sauce
- ☐ 12 ounces spaghetti noodles

Pantry/Spices
- ☐ Flour
- ☐ Onion salt

- ☐ Salt
- ☐ Pepper
- ☐ Chili powder
- ☐ Dry mustard
- ☐ Garlic powder
- ☐ Bread crumbs

Meat
- ☐ 1 (3 pound) beef chuck roast
- ☐ 6 slices bacon
- ☐ 5 pounds ground round

Dairy
- ☐ 4 eggs
- ☐ 1 stick butter
- ☐ ½ cup Swiss cheese
- ☐ ½ cup sour cream
- ☐ ¼ pound Cheddar cheese
- ☐ 24 ounces mozzarella cheese
- ☐ 1 cup cottage cheese
- ☐ Parmesan cheese

Other
- ☐ Dressing* for Simple Salad or add ingredients from pages 29 to 32 to make your own dressing
- ☐ _____
- ☐ _____
- ☐ _____
- ☐ _____
- ☐ _____

*These ingredients are for the Simple Salad (pg. 64) which is served with the Spaghetti Pie.

Week Nineteen Menu

NICE CHICKEN AND RICE
SUGAR CARROTS

o

CHICKEN AND MUSHROOMS
GARLIC TIES

o

LAZY CORDON BLEU
ROBUST RICE PILAF

o

HAM AND SWISS CRESCENT POUCHES
POTATO WEDGES

o

BAKED ORANGE-GINGER CHICKEN
POTATO PILE

NICE CHICKEN AND RICE

8 pieces chicken	3 cups Minute rice™
1 can cream of chicken soup	1 can cream of mushroom soup
½ soup can milk	1 package dry onion soup mix

Preheat oven to 350 degrees. Mix soups, milk and rice. Pour into a 9 x 13-inch pan. Top with chicken. Pour soup mix over top. Cover with foil and bake for 2 hours. Serve with Sugar Carrots (page 90). Makes 8 servings.

CHICKEN AND MUSHROOMS

6 boneless, skinless chicken breasts
2 cups sliced mushrooms
1 can cream of mushroom soup
½ cup cooking sherry
1 cup sour cream

Preheat oven to 350 degrees. Sauté mushrooms in a skillet over medium heat. Place chicken in a 9 x 13-inch baking dish. Mix all remaining ingredients together and spread over chicken. Bake for one hour or until chicken is done. Serve with Garlic Ties (below). Makes 6 servings.

GARLIC TIES

1 pound refrigerated breadstick dough
2 tablespoons all-purpose flour
2 tablespoons olive oil
4 garlic cloves, minced
¼ teaspoon coarse salt

Preheat oven to 375 degrees. Spray a baking sheet with nonstick cooking spray. Divide the dough into eight equal pieces. Roll each piece into a 7-inch length and tie into a knot. Transfer to baking sheet. Bake 30-35 minutes or until golden brown. Let cool. Combine oil and garlic in a nonstick skillet, coated with cooking spray, and over medium-low heat cook 2-3 minutes. Brush the garlic-oil mixture evenly over each "knot" and sprinkle with salt. Makes 8 ties.

LAZY CORDON BLEU

6 boneless, skinless chicken breasts
1 can cream of mushroom soup
2 tablespoons water
2 tablespoons dry white wine
4 cups cooked egg noodles
1 cup shredded Swiss cheese, divided
1 cup chopped ham

Brown chicken in butter for 10 minutes. Mix soup, water, wine, ¾ cup cheese and ham in a separate pan and bring to a boil. Add chicken. Cook over low heat for 5-10 minutes or until chicken is done. Cook noodles according to package directions. Place noodles on plates and top with chicken. Sprinkle with remaining Swiss cheese. Salt and pepper to taste. Serve with Robust Rice Pilaf (page 147). Makes 6 servings.

HAM AND SWISS CRESCENT POUCHES

1 cup cooked ham, chopped
1 tablespoon honey mustard
1 cup broccoli florets
1 package refrigerated crescent-roll dough
1 cup shredded Swiss cheese
1 egg white, beaten
½ cup Miracle Whip®

Preheat oven to 375 degrees. Combine ham, broccoli, cheese, Miracle Whip® and mustard in a large bowl, mixing well. Spread dough out. Spread mixture down middle of dough. Cut dough at every 2 inches and fold to seal in filling. Brush dough with beaten egg white. Bake for 30-35 minutes or until golden brown. Serve with Potato Wedges (page 76). Makes 4 pouches.

BAKED ORANGE-GINGER CHICKEN

1/2 cup thawed frozen concentrated orange juice
3 tablespoons grated pared fresh ginger root
2 tablespoons minced, fresh garlic
4 boneless, skinless chicken breasts

In a gallon-size sealable plastic bag, combine orange juice,
ginger and garlic. Add chicken, turning to coat. Seal bag and
refrigerate at least 30 minutes, turning bag occasionally.
Preheat oven to 375 degrees. Spray a shallow baking pan with
nonstick cooking spray. Drain marinade into small saucepan;
bring to a boil. Remove from heat. Place meat on baking pan.
Carefully pour marinade over chicken. Bake 30-40 minutes, or
until chicken is cooked through and no longer pink. Serve
with a Potato Pile (below). Makes 4 servings.

POTATO PILE

¼ cup melted butter
¼ cup water
½ package dry onion soup
5 medium potatoes (unpeeled)

Preheat oven to 350 degrees. Cut scrubbed potatoes into ¼-
inch thick slices. Mix all other ingredients together. Spread a
layer of potatoes in bottom of 2-quart casserole. Top with ⅓ of
the butter/soup packet mixture. Repeat layers twice more.
Bake for 50-60 minutes or until fork
tender. Makes 4-6 servings.

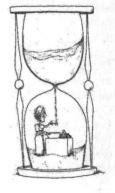

DINNER PLANNING:
Creating Your Own Weekly Menus

In addition to the menus offered in this book, consider creating your own. Each time you prepare a recipe, write down the ingredients, the amounts and number of servings. Somewhere else on the recipe, note which of your family members liked it and then place it in an envelope. I used three different envelopes. In one, I stored recipes that were hands-down family favorites; in the next, those that we liked but wouldn't want to eat every week. The last envelope contained recipes that my husband and I liked but got the thumbs-down from our daughter. Once you have five menus, simply put them in a binder and add a master shopping list. Make as many weekly menus as needed for your family's various tastes.

VARIATION: If creating your own weekly menus sounds too trying, try theme nights. Make Monday night PIZZA NIGHT. Try PASTA NIGHT for Tuesday. Make Wednesday FINGER FOODS. Try BREAKFAST FOR DINNER on Thursdays. Let Friday be TAKEOUT. The options are endless!

GIFT IDEA: If your family has many heirloom recipes, collect them and create several menus as gifts. Add family pictures, journaling and print on attractive paper or take to a copy store for duplication and binding.

Grocery List Week Nineteen

Produce

- ❏ 2 cups mushrooms
- ❏ 6 garlic cloves
- ❏ 1 bunch broccoli
- ❏ Ginger root
- ❏ 5 medium potatoes
- ❏ 1 large package fresh baby carrots*

Breads

- ❏ 1 pound refrigerated bread-stick dough
- ❏ 1 package crescent roll dough

Canned/Boxed Goods

- ❏ 1 can cream of chicken soup
- ❏ 3 cups Minute Rice™
- ❏ 3 cans cream of mushroom soup
- ❏ 2 packages dry onion soup mix
- ❏ ½ cup cooking sherry
- ❏ 2 tablespoons dry white wine
- ❏ Egg noodles
- ❏ Miracle Whip™

Pantry/Spices

- ❏ Flour
- ❏ Brown sugar*
- ❏ Coarse salt
- ❏ Salt
- ❏ Pepper
- ❏ Olive oil

- ❏ Honey mustard
- ❏ Paprika
- ❏ Ketchup or Ranch dressing (to serve with Potato Wedges)

Meat

- ❏ 8 pieces chicken
- ❏ 16 boneless, skinless chicken breasts
- ❏ 2 cups ham, chopped

Dairy

- ❏ Milk
- ❏ 1 cup sour cream
- ❏ 2 cups shredded Swiss cheese
- ❏ 1 egg
- ❏ 1 can frozen orange juice
- ❏ 1 stick butter*

Other

*These ingredients are for the Sugar Carrot side dish (p. 90).

- ❏ _____
- ❏ _____
- ❏ _____
- ❏ _____
- ❏ _____
- ❏ _____
- ❏ _____
- ❏ _____
- ❏ _____
- ❏ _____
- ❏ _____
- ❏ _____
- ❏ _____

3.

INDEX, CHARTS & REFERENCES

WEIGHTS AND MEASURES

A dash = less than ⅛ teaspoon
3 teaspoons = 1 tablespoon
4 tablespoons = ¼ cup
⅓ cup = 5 tablespoons + 1 teaspoon
½ cup = 8 tablespoons
⅔ cup = 10 tablespoons + 2 teaspoons
½ pint = 1 cup
1 quart = 4 cups
4 quarts = 1 gallon
8 ounces = 1 cup liquid
8 ounces = ½ pound
16 ounces = 2 pints or ½ quart liquid
16 ounces = 1 pound
32 ounces = 1 quart
64 ounces = ½ gallon
1 liter = 1.06 quarts
1 quart = .95 liter

YIELDS AND EQUIVALENTS

Apple	1 medium, chopped=about 1 cup
	3 medium=1 pound or 2 and ¾ cups, sliced
Bacon	½ cup crumbled=8 slices crisply cooked
Bananas	3 large or 4 small=2 cups sliced or 1 ⅓ cups mashed
Beans, dried	1 cup =2¼ to 2 and ½ cups cooked
Beef, cooked	1 cup ½ inch pieces=5 ounces
Butter	1 ounce butter=2 tablespoons
	1 stick butter= ¼ pound or 8 ounces
	1 cup butter=2 sticks or ½ pound
Celery	2 medium stalks=⅔ to ¾ cup
Cheese	1 pound=4 cups shredded
	1 cup shredded=¼ pound
	2 cups cottage cheese=16 ounces
	6 tablespoons cream cheese=3 ounces
Cherries	½ pound=1 cup pitted
Chocolate	1 ounce=1 square
	1 cup chips=6 ounces
Cranberries	1 cup fresh makes 1 cup sauce
	1 pound=4 cups
Crumbs	1 cup cracker crumbs=28 saltine crackers
	1 cup graham cracker crumbs=14 square graham crackers
	1 cup cracker crumbs=24 rich round crackers
	1 cup bread crumbs=1½ slices fresh or 4 slices dry
	1 cup vanilla wafer crumbs=22 wafers
	1 cup chocolate wafer crumbs=19 wafers
Eggs	1 cup=4 large eggs
	½ cup liquid egg substitute=1 egg
	1 cup egg yolks=10 to 12 egg yolks
	1 cup egg whites=8 to 10 egg whites
Garlic	1 clove fresh=½ teaspoon chopped or ⅛ teaspoon garlic powder
Grapes	1 pound=2 cups halved
Green Pepper	1 large=1 cup diced
Herbs	1 tablespoon fresh, snipped=1 teaspoon dried or ½ teaspoon ground
Lemon	Juice of 1 lemon=3 tablespoons
	Grated peel of 1 lemon=about 1 teaspoon
Lettuce	6 cups bite-size pieces=1-pound head
Macaroni	1 to 1 and ¼ cups=4 ounces or 2 to 2½ cups
	Cooked—16 ounces=about 8 cups cooked
Marshmallows	10 miniature=1 large
	1 cup=11 large
Mushrooms (Fresh)	8 ounces= 2 and ½ cups sliced or 1 cup cooked
	1 cup sliced and cooked=4 ounce can, drained
Mustard	1 teaspoon dry=1 tablespoon prepared

Nuts	1 cup chopped=¼ pound or 4 ounces
	1 cup whole or halved= 4 to 5 ounces
Oats	1¾ cups cooked=1 cup raw
Olives	24 small=2 ounces=about ½ cup sliced
Onions	1 medium, chopped= ½ cup
	1 medium=1 teaspoon onion powder or 1 tablespoon dried minced
Orange	Juice of one orange=⅓ to ½ cup
	Grated peel of 1 orange=2 tablespoons
Peaches/Pears	1 medium= ½ cup sliced
Potatoes	3 medium=2 cups sliced or cubed
	3 medium=1¾ cups mashed
Rice	1 cup white rice (long grain)=about 7 ounces=3 to 4 cups cooked
	1 cup white rice(instant)=2 cups cooked
	1 cup brown rice=3 cups cooked
	1 cup wild rice=3 to 4 cups cooked
	1 pound cooked wild rice=2⅔ cup dry
Sour cream	1 cup=8 ounces
Spaghetti and Noodles	
	8 ounces=4 cups cooked
	1 pound=8 cups cooked
Strawberries	1 quart=2 cups sliced
Sugar	Powdered 4 cups=1 pound
	Brown 2¼ cups, packed=1 pound
	Granulated 2 cups=1 pound
Tomatoes	1 cup canned=1⅓ cups fresh, cut up
Whipping Cream	1 cup=2 cups whipped
Yeast	1 package=2¼ teaspoon regular or quick active dry

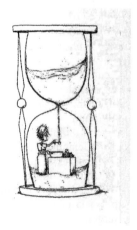

EMERGENCY SUBSTITUTIONS

Baking Powder: 1 teaspoon=½ teaspoon cream of tartar plus ¼ teaspoon baking soda

Balsamic Vinegar: Sherry or cider vinegar

Beer: Apple juice or beef broth

Broth: 1 teaspoon granulated or 1 cube bouillon dissolved in one cup water

Brown Sugar, Packed: Equal amount of granulated sugar

Buttermilk: 1 teaspoon lemon juice or vinegar plus milk to make 1 cup; let stand 5 minutes

Cajun Seasoning: Equal parts white pepper, black pepper, ground red pepper, onion powder, garlic powder and paprika

Chocolate: For 1 square, unsweetened: 3 tablespoons cocoa plus 1 tablespoon butter.
For 1 square semisweet: 1 square unsweetened+1 tablespoon sugar
For 2 squares, semisweet: ⅓ cup semisweet chips

Corn Syrup: For light or dark: 1 cup + ¼ cup water
For dark: 1 cup light corn syrup or 1 cup maple syrup or ¾ light corn syrup + ¼ cup molasses

Cornstarch: For 1 tablespoon: 2 tablespoons all-purpose flour

Cream of Mushroom: For one can: 1 cup thick white sauce + 4 ounce can mushrooms, drained and chopped

Eggs: For 1 egg: 2 egg whites or 2 egg yolks or ¼ cup liquid egg substitute

Flour: Cake flour: 1 cup minus 2 tablespoons all-purpose flour.
Self-rising: 1 cup all-purpose flour + 1 teaspoon baking powder and ½ teaspoon salt.

Honey: 1¼ cup sugar ¼ cup water

Leeks: Equal amounts green onions or shallots

Lemon Juice: For 1 teaspoon: 1 teaspoon cider vinegar or white vinegar

Milk: ½ cup evaporated (not condensed) milk plus ½ cup water

Molasses: Equal amount honey

Mushrooms: For 1 cup cooked: 4 ounce can, drained

Poultry Seasoning: For 1 teaspoon: ¾ teaspoon sage + ¼ teaspoon thyme

Pumpkin Pie Spice: For 1 teaspoon: ½ teaspoon cinnamon + ¼ teaspoon ground ginger + ⅛ teaspoon ground allspice + ⅛ teaspoon ground nutmeg

Red Pepper Sauce:	4 drops=⅛ teaspoon ground cayenne(red) pepper
Sour Cream:	Equal amount of plain yogurt
Tomato sauce:	For 2 cups sauce: ¾ cups paste + 1and ¼ cup water
Wine: For white:	apple juice, apple cider, white grape juice, chicken or vegetable broth, water
For red:	apple cider, chicken, beef or vegetable broth, water
Yogurt:	equal amounts of sour cream

FREEZER STORAGE

Breads, Baked   2 to 3 months
Cakes   3 to 4 months
Cookies   3 to 4 months

Dairy Products:
Butter or Margarine   9 to 12 months
Cottage Cheese   3 months
Cream   1 to 4 months
Hard Natural Cheese   6 months
Processed Cheese   3 months
Soft cheese   6 months
Yogurt   1 to 2 months

Eggs:
Whole eggs   Do not freeze
Egg yolks (cover in water)   6 months
Egg whites   6 months
Egg substitute   6 months

Fruits/Juices   8 to 12 months

Meats:
Beef, roasts or steaks   6 months
Beef, ground   3 months
Beef, stew meat   3 to 6 months
Lamb   6 months
Pork, roast or chops   3 to 6 months
Pork, ground   2 months
Veal   6 months
Cured meat, ham or bacon   1 to 2 months
Hot dogs   1 to 2 months

Sausages	2 to 3 months
Poultry, pieces	6 months
Poultry, whole	1 year
Fish-fatty (salmon, mackerel, trout)	2 months
Fish-lean (cod, haddock, pike)	6 months
Fish-breaded, cooked	2 to 3 months
Shellfish	2 to 4 months
Pies, Baked or Pie shells	4 months
Pies, unbaked	2 months
Nuts, shelled	3 months
Vegetables	8 months

Cooked Foods:

Casseroles	3 months
Meat	1 to 3 months
Soups	4 months

REFRIGERATOR STORAGE

(Always check dates on package before purchasing)

Breads	5 to 7 days
Condiments	12 months

Dairy:

Buttermilk	2 weeks
Eggs, whole	1 week
Eggs, yolks or whites	2 to 4 days
Sour cream	2 weeks
Yogurt	2 weeks
Cottage Cheese	10 to 30 days
Cream Cheese	2 weeks
Hard Cheese	3 to 4 weeks
Sliced Cheese	2 weeks
Spread Cheese	1 to 2 weeks
Cream, heavy	3 to 5 days
Cream, half-and-half	3 to 5 days
Milk	5-7 days
Butter	2 weeks
Margarine	1 month
Mayonnaise	6 months
Salad Dressings (purchased)	6 months
Salad Dressings (homemade)	3-7 days

Fruit:

Apples	1 month
Apricots	3 to 5 days

Avocados	3 to 5 days
Berries	2 to 3 days
Cranberries	1 week
Citrus fruits	2 weeks
Dried fruits	6 months
Grapes	3 to 5 days
Melons	3 to 5 days
Peaches	3 to 5 days
Pears	3 to 5 days
Pineapple	2 to 3 days
Plums	3 to 5 days

Meat, Poultry, Seafood:
Fresh:

Chops	3 to 5 days
Ground meats	1 to 2 days
Roasts	3 to 5 days
Steaks	3 to 5 days

Processed:

Cold cuts (unopened)	2 weeks
Cold cuts (opened)	3 to 5 days
Cured bacon	1 week
Hot dogs	1 week
Ham-sliced	3 to 5 days
Ham-whole	1 week
Poultry/Seafood	1 to 2 days

Vegetables:

Asparagus	2 to 3 days
Broccoli	3 to 5 days
Cabbage	2 weeks
Carrots	2 weeks
Cauliflower	1 week
Celery	1 week
Corn, sweet	1 day
Cucumbers	1 week
Green Beans	1 week
Green Onions	3 to 5 days
Green Peas	3 to 5 days
Green Peppers	1 week
Lettuce	3 to 5 days
Radishes	2 weeks
Tomatoes	1 week
Squash	3 to 5 days

NOTES:

NOTES:

ALPHABETICAL INDEX

A

Almost Oriental Noodle Dish, 69
Applesauce, 127
Attitude, 24

B

Balsamic Vinaigrette Dressing, 32
Berry-Good Fruit Parfaits, 35
Beans—
-Instant Tacos, 41
Bean-less Tacos, 41
Beef—
-Almost Oriental Noodle Dish, 69
-Cajun Flank Steak, 175
-Christmas-Eve Chili, 93
-Enchilada Casserole, 174
-Famous Fiesta Casserole, 64
-French Dips, 43
-Ground Beef Pita Pizza, 187
-Italian pasta skillet, 42
-Hamburger Club, 294
-Kid-Friendly Sloppy Joes, 75
-Kids-Love-It Casserole, 148
-Marinated Flank Steak, 184
-Marvelous Meatloaf, 153
-Tips for, 157
-Beef Mix, 38
-Mushroom and Beef Pasta, 155
-Pot Roast Perfection, 112
-Really Good, Creative Tacos, 166
-Roast Beef & Gravy, 198
-Salisbury Steak, 125
 - Speedy, 125
-Samantha's Favorite Noodle
 Bake, 95
-Shepherd's Pie, 113
-Shredded Beef Sandwiches, 175
-Stroganoff, 104
 - Hip & Healthy, 152
-Taco Pizza, 148
-Toast-burgers, 40
Beef Mix, 38
B.L.T. Pita, 63
Breakfast, 23, 27-28

-Balanced breakfast, 27
-Breakfast ideas, 28
-For dinner, 43
Bread—
-Biscuits, 126
-Garlic Ties, 206
-I-Slaved-All-Day-Biscuits, 126
-Parmesan Garlic Toasts, 177
-Ricotta-Pesto, 168
-Tomato, 124
Breadsticks—
-Bedazzling, 133
-Choose-a-Way, 202
-Garlic Ties, 206
-Tips for, 102
Broccoli—
-Broccoli Bake, 198
-Rosemary, 134
Broiled Melbas, 36
Bulk cooking, 37
Carrots—
-Sugar, 90
-Sweet and Sour, 113
Biscuits, 126
Cajun—
-Chicken 161
-Flank Steak, 184
Casseroles—
-Basil Chicken with Wild Rice, 194
-Beef Enchilada Casserole, 174
-Broccoli Bake, 198
-Cheddar-y Turkey Casserole, 153
-Chicken and Vegetable Bake, 126
-Chicken Ricotta Pasta Bake, 185
-Classic Chicken Bake, 90
-Crazy Corn Casserole, 192
-Fiesta, 187
-Ham and Pasta Bake, 160
-Gnarly-Barley Casserole, 163
-Kids-Love-It Casserole, 148
-Nice Chicken and Rice, 206
-Spaghetti Pie, 203
-Toss-it-Together Lasagna, 201
-Turkey and Stuffing Casserole,
 105

C

Cinnamon Chips, 36
Chicken—
  -Baked Orange Ginger Chicken, 208
  -Basil Chicken with Wild Rice, 100
  -Chicken and Cheese Enchiladas, 194
  -Chicken Broth with Angel-Hair Pasta, 167
  -Chicken Fettuccini Dijon, 127
  -Chicken & Potatoes Skillet, 68
  -Chicken and Ravioli, 42
  -Chicken Ricotta Pasta Bake, 185
  -Chicken & Vegetable Bake, 126
  -Classic Chicken Bake, 90
  -Caesar Salad, 92
  -Cajun Chicken, 161
  -Chicken and Mushrooms, 206
  -Cordon Bleu, 160
  -Covered Chicken, 68
  -Cool and Crispy Chicken, 115
  -Delightfully Dijon Chicken, 103
  -Gnarly Barley Casserole, 167
  -Grilled Honey Chicken, 142
  -In "Whine" Sauce, 78
  -Italian Chicken in a Flash, 147
  -Lazy Cordon Bleu, 207
  -Lemon-Broiled Chicken, 168
  -Let-me-Soak Chicken, 96
  -Nice Chicken and Rice, 206
  -Quesadilla Bites, 85
  -Quick & Crispy, 60
  -Perfect Parmesan Chicken, 146
  -Parmesan, 135
  -Stroganoff, 70
  -Speedy Fajitas, 184
  -Taco Revival, 198
  -Tenders, 82
    --adult version, 82
Chili, 93
  -freezing, 93
  -jalapenos in, 94
Clutter, 135
Cobbler, (awesome apple), 176
Cookies—
  -Almond Bites, 53
  -Shooting Stars, 53

Cooking for Blondes, 31-32
Corn—
  -on the Cob, 83
  -Crazy Corn Casserole, 192
  -Fiesta, 187
Coupons, 155
Creamy Buttermilk Dressing, 31
Creamy Garlic & Chive Dressing, 30
Creamy Italian Dressing, 30
Croutons, make your own – 122

D

Delightfully Dijon Chicken, 103
Dessert—
  -Almond Bites, 53
  -Any-Berry Sauce, 52
  -Awesome Apple Cobbler, 176
  -Bananas Foster, 52
    --serving ideas for, 52
  -Bananarama Cream Pie, 47
  -Berry Compote, 132
  -Cinnamon Baked Apples, 179
  -Crispy Peanut Butter Chocolate Pie, 47
  -Crispy Cinnamon Sundae, 51
  -Darlene's Five Minute Fudge, 51
  -Fruit Pizza, 48
  -Fondue for You, 49
  -Hot Fudge Mocha Shake, 48
  -Minute Meringue, 46
  -Quick Cherry Tarts, 46
  -Simple Strawberry Shortcake, 50
  -Shooting Stars, 53
  -Snicker Bar Surprise, 50
  -Vanilla Berry Dream, 49
Dressings—
  -Balsamic Vinaigrette, 32
  -Creamy Buttermilk, 31
  -Creamy Garlic & Chive, 30
  -Creamy Italian, 30
  -Fresh and Fruity, 31
  -Lemon-Garlic Vinaigrette, 32
  -Orange-Dijon, 29
  -Preparation, 30
  -Smokey-Tomato Dressing, 32
  -Super-Citrus, 29

-Sweet and Sour, 31
-Tips for, 92

E

Easy Pasta Toss, 61
Eggs—
  -Scrumptious Swiss-Strata, 77
Enchiladas—
  -Chicken and Cheese, 186
  -Enchilada Casserole, 188
Exercise, 24-25

F

Fajitas, (chicken)
Finger-Paints (edible), 154
Five Rules (of Rush Hour recipes),
  19
French Bread Pizzas, 70
French Dips, 43
Fresh and Fruity Dressing, 31
Freezer cooking, 37
Fruit—
  -Aunt Joan's Fruit Cup, 102
  -Awesome Apple Cobbler, 176
  -Berry Compote, 132
  -Cinnamon Baked Apples, 179
  -Fruit Pizza, 48
Fruit Salad
  -Pretty Peach Cup, 114
  -Slicing, 114
Frozen Assets, 37
Fudge, 51

G

Green Beans, (Glorious), 86
  -preparation of, 86
Grilled Cheese, 162
Grocery Shopping, 84
Ground beef, (see beef)

H

Ham—
  -Ham and Cheese Pita, 63
  -Ham and Crescent Pouches, 207
  -Ham and Pasta Bake, 160
  -Ham and Potatoes, 140
  -Ham and Swiss Pizza, 61
  -Hammy Noodles, 141
Healthy choices, 26
Healthy eating, 21
How to use this book, 5

I

Instant family dinners, 40-43
Instant Tacos, 41
Italian Marinade, 33
Italian Pasta Skillet, 42

L

Lasagna—
  Lasagna Rolls, 132
  -freezing, 134
  -Toss-it-Together Lasagna, 201
Lemon Angel-Hair Pasta, 193
Lemon-Garlic Vinaigrette Dressing,
  32
Linguini with Herb Butter, 193
Lunch, 23

M

Macaroni—
  -Magnificent, 114
  -Presto Mac, 91
Manicotti, (cheese-stuffed), 170
Marinades—
  -Italian, 33
  -Red Wine, 33
  -Rosemary-Basil, 33
  -White Wine, 33
Mash-It Potatoes, 60
Meatballs, 38
Meatloaf, 38
  -Marvelous, 153
  -Tips for, 153
Menu plans, 8-12
Mozzarella Sticks, 130
Mushrooms—
  -and beef pasta, 155
  -and chicken, 206
Marvelous Rice, 156
  -Tips about, 156

N

Nachos, 74
Noodles—see pasta

O

Orange-Dijon Dressing, 29

P

Pancakes—
-Ideas for, 27
-Perfectly Pleasing, 39
Pasta—
-Almost Oriental Noodles Dish, 69
-Basic Fettuccini, 162
-Bowtie Bonanza, 124
-Cheese-Stuffed Manicotti, 170
-freezing, 170
-Chicken Fettuccini Dijon, 127
-Coloring, 61
-Ham and Pasta Bake, 160
-Hammy Noodles, 141
-Hints and Tips, 91
-Italian Pasta Skillet, 42
-Lasagna Rolls, 132
- freezing, 132
-Toss it Together Lasagna, 201
-Lemon Angel-Hair Pasta, 193
-Linguini with Herb Butter, 193
-Magnificent Mac, 114
-Mushroom and Beef, 155
-No-Red-Sauce Spaghetti, 141
-Noodle Bake, 177
-Parmesan Rotini, 82
-Presto Mac, 91
-Presto Pasta, 102
-Pretty Pasta Salad, 75
-Rockin' Rotini, 134
-Sals-a-Roni, 41
-Samantha's Favorite Noodle Bake, 95
-Sour Cream Pasta, 103
-Soy-Sketti, 155
-Spaghetti Pie, 203
-Stand-By Spaghetti Sauce, 106
Pies—
-Bananarama Cream Pie, 47
-Crispy Peanut Butter Chocolate Pie, 47
Pita—
-B.L.T. Pita, 63
-Calzone, Sandwich, 63
-Ground Beef Pita Pizza, 193
-Ham & Cheese Pita, 63
-"Pita" Soup, 62
-Taco Pita, 63
-Veggie Pita, 63
Pork—
-Chili Tortilla Pie, 167
-Shake and Bake It, 40
-Tuscan-Style Pork Roast, 178
Pork Chops—
-Honey Chops, 122
-Perfect, 85
-Stacked, 140
Potatoes—
-Aunt Sally's, 135
-Baked, 116
-Baked Potato Bonanza, 116
-Baking tips, 115
-Cheesy-Scalloped Spuds, 97
-Cinnamon Sweet, 112
-Dijon, 85
-Funky Fries, 163
-Lyonnaise, 169
-Mash-It, 60
-Tips for mashed, 60
-Pancakes, 154
-Perfect Parmesan, 146
-Pile, 208
-Poupon, 78
-Ranch, 125
-Squares, 199
-Sweet Potatoes, 112
-Twice-Baked, 161
-Wedges, 76
-With Ham, 140
Pot Roast Perfection, 112
Pizza—
-Burgers, 200
-Cheese Pizza Please, 149
-Dough options, 151
-French Bread, 70
-Ground Beef Pita Pizza, 187
-Generic, 43
-Ham and Swiss, 61

-Taco, 148
Presto Primavera, 83
Pretty Peach Cup, 114

Q

Quesadilla Bites, 84
Quick and Crispy Chicken, 60

R

Red Wine Marinade, 33
Rice—
  -Marvelous Mushroom, 156
  -Robust Rice Pilaf, 147
  -Twice as Nice Veggie Rice, 123
  -Wild, 200
Rush Hour Cook Club, 20
Rosemary-Basil Marinade, 33

S

Salads—
  -Pretty Pasta, 75
  -Tips for, 75
  -Simple, 64
  -Taco-Nacho, 74
  -Very Garlic-y Caesar, 92
Salad dressings (see dressings)
Salisbury Steak, 125
  - speedy, 125
Sals-a-Roni, 41
Sandwiches—(also see pitas and
  pizzas)
  -Kid-Friendly Sloppy Joes, 75
  -Grilled Cheese, 162
  -Ground Beef Pita Pizza, 187
  -Hamburger Club, 194
  -Ham and Crescent Pouches, 207
  -Make Mine A Melt, 76
  -Pitas—
    -B.L.T. Pita, 63
    -Ground Beef Pita Pizza, 187
    -Ham & Cheese Pita, 63
    -"Pita" Soup, 62
    -Taco Pita, 63
    -Veggie Pita, 63
    -Pita Calzone, 63
    -Pizza Burgers, 200

-Shredded Beef, 175
Scalloped Potatoes, 97
Shake It and Bake It, 40
Shepherd's Pie, 112
Sloppy Joes, 75
Smoked Tomato Dressing, 31
Sour Cream Pasta, 103
Snacks—
  -Berry-Good Fruit Parfaits, 35
  -Broiled Melbas, 36
  -Cinnamon Chips, 36
  -Ideas for, 34
  -Pita Crisps, 35
  -Stocking up, 34
Soups—
  -Angel-Hair, 167
  -"Pita," 62
  -Steak, 117
Spices, 117
  -make your own, 165
Steaming Vegetables, 44
Scrumptious Swiss Strata, 77
Stroganoff—
  -Beef, 104, 152
  -Chicken, 70
  -Hip & Healthy, 156
  -Tips for, 104
Super-Citrus Dressing, 29
Smoothies
  -Another Fruit, 55
  -Berry Surprise, 54
  -Bodacious Banana & Blueberry
    55
  -Chocolate Banana, 56
  -Coffee-nana Smoothie, 55
  -Healthy, 55
  -Instant O.J. Smoothie, 56
  -Just Like-Frap, 56
  -Orange Frosty, 54
  -The Rush Hour Cook's, 27
  -Watermelon Wonders, 56
Spaghetti, 106
  -No Red Sauce, 141
  -Pie, 203
Sauce for, 107
  -freezing, 107
  -vegetarian, 107
Sweet and Sour Dressing, 31

T

Tacos, 172, 41
Taco Pita, 63
Taco Pizza, 150
Taco Revival, 192
Taco Nachos, 74
Taco Salad, 74
Toast-Burgers, 40
Turkey—
  -2+2+2+2=Turkey, 86
  -Cheddar-y Turkey Casserole, 153
  -Tasty Turkey Slices, 130
  -Turkey and Stuffing Casserole,
    105
  -Turkey Pot Pie, 131

V

Vegetables—
  -As appetizers, 69
  -Broccoli—
    -Broccoli Bake, 198
    -Rosemary, 134
  -Corn—
    -Corn on the Cob, 83
  -Crazy Corn Casserole, 192
  -Fiesta Corn, 187
Five-a-Day, 133
Glorious Green Beans, 86
  -preparation, 86
How to eat, 45
  Mushrooms—
    -and beef pasta, 159
    -and chicken, 219
    -Marvelous Rice, 160
    -Tips about, 160
Onion tips, 123
Pita Sandwich, 63
Raw Rule, 69
Steaming success, 44
Sugar Carrots, 90
Sweet and Sour Carrots, 113

W

Weight issues, 22
Waffles, 28
White Wine Marinade, 33
Women in Wellness, 21

MAKE YOUR OWN MENU INDEX

Use this index to choose a main course, side dish and dessert to build your own weekly menu!
There is also an alphabetical index on page 221.
For a quick glance at complete weekly plans, please see pages 8-12.
NOTE: Some recipes appear under more than one category.

CHICKEN DISHES

Baked Orange Ginger Chicken, 208
Basil Chicken with Wild Rice, 194
Chicken and Cheese Enchiladas, 186
Chicken Fettuccini Dijon, 127
Chicken & Potatoes Skillet, 68
Chicken Ricotta Pasta Bake, 185
Chicken Stroganoff, 70
Chicken Tenders, 82
Chicken & Vegetable Bake, 126
Classic Chicken Bake, 90
Cajun Chicken, 161
Chicken and Mushrooms, 206
Chicken and Ravioli, 42
Cordon Bleu, 164
Covered Chicken, 68
Cool and Crispy Chicken, 115
Delightfully Dijon Chicken, 103
Gnarly Barley Casserole, 163
Grilled Honey Chicken, 142
In "Whine" Sauce, 78
Italian Chicken in a Flash, 147
Lazy Cordon Bleu, 207
Lemon-Broiled Chicken, 168
Let-me-Soak Chicken, 96
Nice Chicken and Rice, 206
Quesadilla Bites, 85
Quick & Crispy Chicken, 60
Perfect Parmesan Chicken, 146
Parmesan Chicken, 135
Speedy Chicken Fajitas, 184
Taco Revival, 198

HAM DISHES

Ham and Pasta Bake, 160
Ham and Potatoes, 140
Hammy Noodles, 141

TURKEY DISHES

2+2+2+2=Turkey, 86
Cheddar-y Turkey Casserole, 153
Tasty Turkey Slices, 130
Turkey and Stuffing Casserole, 105
Turkey Pot Pie, 131

ENTREE SALADS

Very Garlic-y Caesar Salad, 92
Taco-Nacho Salad, 74

PIZZA DISHES

Pizza Burgers, 200
Cheese Pizza Please, 149
French Bread Pizza, 70
Ground Beef Pita Pizza, 187
Generic Pizza, 43
Ham and Swiss Pizza, 61
Taco Pizza, 148

PORK DISHES

Chili Tortilla Pie, 167
Pork Chops—
   -Honey Chops, 122
   -Perfect, 85
   -Stacked, 140
Tuscan-Style Pork Roast, 178

CASSEROLES

Basil Chicken with Wild Rice, 194
Beef Enchilada Casserole, 174
Broccoli Bake, 198
Cheddar-y Turkey Casserole, 153
Chicken and Vegetable Bake, 126
Chicken Ricotta Pasta Bake, 185
Classic Chicken Bake, 90
Ham and Pasta Bake, 160
Gnarly-Barley Casserole, 163

Kids-Love-It Casserole, 148
Nice Chicken and Rice, 206
Scrumptious Swiss Strata, 77
Spaghetti Pie, 203
Shepherd's Pie, 113
Toss-it-Together Lasagna, 201
Turkey and Stuffing Casserole,
   105

BEEF DISHES
Almost Oriental Noodle Dish, 69
Beef Mix, 38
Cajun Flank Steak, 175
Christmas-Eve Chili, 93
Enchilada Casserole, 174
Famous Fiesta Casserole, 64
Italian pasta skillet, 42
Kids-Love-It Casserole, 148
Marinated Flank Steak, 184
Marvelous Meatloaf, 153
Mushroom and Beef Pasta, 155
Pot Roast Perfection, 112
Really Good, Creative Tacos, 166
Roast Beef & Gravy, 198
Salisbury Steak, 125
Samantha's Favorite Noodle Bake,
   95
Shepherd's Pie, 113
Beef Stroganoff, 104, 152

PASTA DISHES
Almost Oriental Noodles Dish, 69
Basic Fettuccini, 162
Bowtie Bonanza, 124
Cheese-Stuffed Manicotti, 170
Chicken and Ravioli, 42
Chicken Broth with Angel-Hair
   Pasta, 167
Chicken Fettuccini Dijon, 127
Easy Pasta Toss, 61
Ham and Pasta Bake, 160
Hammy Noodles, 141
Italian Pasta Skillet, 42
Lasagna Rolls, 132
Toss it Together Lasagna, 201
Lemon Angel-Hair Pasta, 193
Linguini with Herb Butter, 193
Magnificent Mac, 114

Mushroom and Beef, 155
No-Red-Sauce Spaghetti, 141
Noodle Bake, 177
Parmesan Rotini, 82
Presto Mac, 91
Presto Pasta, 102
Presto Primavera, 83
Pretty Pasta Salad, 75
Rockin' Rotini, 134
Sals-a-Roni, 41
Samantha's Favorite Noodle
   Bake, 95
Soy-Sketti, 155
Spaghetti Pie, 203
Stand-By Spaghetti Sauce, 106
Super Sauce for Spaghetti, 107

MARINADES
Italian, 33
Red Wine, 33
Rosemary-Basil, 33
White Wine, 33

SANDWICHES
Kid-Friendly Sloppy Joes, 75
French Dips, 43
Grilled Cheese, 162
Ground Beef Pita Pizza, 187
Hamburger Club, 194
Ham and Crescent Pouches, 207
Make Mine A Melt, 76
Pitas—
  -B.L.T. Pita, 63
  -Ham & Cheese Pita, 63
  -Taco Pita, 63
  -Veggie Pita, 63
Pita Calzone, 63
Pizza Burgers, 200
Shredded Beef Sandwiches, 175
Toast-Burgers, 40

SNACKS
Berry-Good Fruit Parfaits, 35
Broiled Melbas, 36
Cinnamon Chips, 36
Pita Crisps, 35

SMOOTHIES

Another Fruit, 55
Berry Surprise, 54
Bodacious Banana & Blueberry, 55
Chocolate Banana, 56
Coffee-nana, 55
Healthy, 55
Instant O.J., 56
Just-Like-Frap, 56
Orange Frosty, 54
The Rush Hour Cook's Favorite
   Smoothie, 27
Watermelon Wonders, 56

COOKIES AND DESSERTS

Cookies—
 Almond Bites, 53
 Shooting Stars, 53
Desserts—
Any-Berry Sauce, 52
Awesome Apple Cobbler, 176
Bananas Foster, 52
Bananarama Cream Pie, 47
Berry Compote, 132
Berry-Good Fruit Parfaits, 35
Cinnamon Baked Apples, 179
Crispy Peanut Butter Chocolate Pie,
 47
Crispy Cinnamon Sundae, 51
Darlene's Five Minute Fudge, 51
Fruit Pizza, 48
Fondue for You, 49
Hot Fudge Mocha Shake, 48
Minute Meringue, 46
Quick Cherry Tarts, 46
Simple Strawberry Shortcakes, 50
Snicker Bar Surprise, 50
Vanilla Berry Dream, 49

SALAD DRESSINGS

Balsamic Vinaigrette, 32
Creamy Buttermilk, 31
Creamy Garlic & Chive, 30
Creamy Italian, 30
Fresh and Fruity, 31
Lemon-Garlic Vinaigrette, 32
Orange-Dijon, 29
Smokey-Tomato Dressing, 32
Super-Citrus, 29
Sweet and Sour, 31

SIDE DISHES / FRUIT

Aunt Joan's Fruit Cup, 102
Awesome Applesauce, 127
Cinnamon Baked Apples, 179
Fruit Pizza, 48
Fruit Salad, 59
Pretty Peach Cup, 114

SIDE DISHES / BREADS

Garlic Ties, 206
I-Slaved-All-Day-Biscuits, 126
Parmesan Garlic Toasts, 177
Ricotta-Pesto Bread, 168
Tomato Bread, 124
Breadsticks—
   -Bedazzling, 133
   -Choose-a-Way, 202

SIDE DISHES / SOUPS AND CHILI

Chicken Broth with Angel Hair
   Pasta, 167
Chili, 93
"Pita" Soup, 62
Steak Soup, 117

SIDE DISHES / VEGETABLES

Broccoli Bake, 198
Rosemary Broccoli, 134
Corn on the Cob, 83
Crazy Corn Casserole, 192
Fiesta Corn, 872
Glorious Green Beans, 86
Marvelous Mushroom Rice, 156
Sugar Carrots, 90
Sweet and Sour Carrots, 113

SIDE DISHES / RICE

Marvelous Mushroom Rice, 156
Robust Rice Pilaf, 147
Twice as Nice Veggie Rice, 123

SIDE DISHES / SALADS

Very Garlic-y Caesar Salad, 92
Pretty Pasta Salad, 75
Simple Salad, 64
Taco-Nacho Salad, 74

SIDE DISHES / POTATOES

Aunt Sally's Potatoes, 135
Baked Potato Bonanza, 116
Cheesy-Scalloped Spuds, 97
Cinnamon Sweet Potatoes, 112
Dijon Potatoes, 85
Funky Fries, 163
Lyonnaise Potatoes, 169
Mash-It Potatoes, 60

Potato Pancakes, 154
Perfect Parmesan Potatoes, 146
Potato Pile, 208
Poupon Potatoes, 78
Ranch Potatoes, 125
Potato Squares, 199
Sweet Potatoes, 112
Twice-Baked Potatoes, 161
Potato Wedges, 76

SIDE DISHES / PASTA

Basic Fettuccini, 162
Easy Pasta Toss, 61
Lemon Angel-Hair Pasta, 193
Linguini with Herb Butter, 193
Parmesan Rotini, 82
Pretty Pasta Salad, 75
Rockin' Rotini, 134
Sour Cream Pasta, 102

Checkout these online services brought to you by Champion Press, Ltd.

WWW.RUSHHOURCOOK.COM

Quick recipes.
Fun trivia.
Real advice.
Join the free "Daily Rush" cooking club.

THE FIVE RULES OF RUSH HOUR RECIPES:

1. All ingredients may be pronounced accurately through the phonetic use of the English Language.

2. Each ingredient can be located in the market without engaging on a full-scale scavenger hunt.

3. No list of ingredients shall be longer than the instructions.

4. Each recipe is durable enough to survive the Queen-of-Incapable Cooking and elicit a compliment.

5. The Rush Hour Cook's finicky child will eat it—or some portion of it.

> HOW TO CONTACT THE RUSH HOUR COOK
> Write to brook@rushhourcook.com
> or 4308 Blueberry Road
> Fredonia WI 53021

Women in Wellness

www.womeninwellness.com

IT'S ALL ABOUT YOU!
fitness...with a twist

What's different about Women in Wellness?

1. A whole-approach to wellness, covering physical, emotional and spiritual health
2. Interactive one-on-one coaching and customized planning
3. Sisters in Success support program
4. We give you points, redeemable for prizes as you reach your goals!

change your life with a click...
visit us today for a free 30 day trial!

Also available from Champion Press, Ltd.

by Brook Noel a.k.a. The Rush Hour Cook
The Rush Hour Cook: Family Favorites by Brook Noel $5.95
The Rush Hour Cook: One-Pot Wonders by Brook Noel $5.95
The Rush Hour Cook: Effortless Entertaining by Brook Noel $5.95
The Rush Hour Cook: Presto Pasta by Brook Noel $5.95
The Rush Hour Cook:; Weekly Wonders $16

by Deborah Taylor-Hough
Frozen Assets: Cook for a Day, Eat for a Month $14.95
Frozen Assets Lite & Easy: Cook for a Day, Eat for a Month $14.95
Frozen Assets Readers' Favorites $25
Mix and Match Recipes: Creative Recipes for Busy Kitchens $9.95

The Complete Crockpot Cookbook: Spectacular Meals for Your Slow Cooker by Wendy Louise *$16*

Cooking for Blondes: gourmet recipes for the culinarily challenged by Rhonda Levtich $27.95/hardcover $16/paperback

365 Quick, Easy and Inexpensive Dinner Menus by Penny E. Stone (Over 1000 recipes!) $19.95

The Frantic Family Cookbook: mostly healthy meals in minutes by Leanne Ely $29.95 hardcover, $14.95 paperback

Healthy Foods: an irreverent guide to understanding nutrition and feeding your family well by Leanne Ely $19.95

Crazy About Crockpots: 101 Easy & Inexpensive Recipes for Less than .75 cents a serving by Penny Stone $12

Crazy About Crockpots: 101 Soups & Stews for Less than .75 cents a serving by Penny Stone $12

Crazy About Crockpots: 101 Recipes for Entertaining at Less than .75 cents a serving by Penny Stone $12

TO ORDER
read excerpts, sample recipes, order books and more at
www.championpress.com

or send a check payable to Champion Press, Ltd. to 4308 Blueberry Road, Fredonia, WI 53021. Please include $3.95 shipping & handling for the first item and $1 for each additional item. Wisconsin residents add .056 for state sales tax.

Lifepath

a new website
offering e-courses to
improve your life…

you'll find expert instruction and personal
coaching on…

☐ emotional wellness
☐ health and nutrition
☐ creativity
☐ writing and journaling
☐ work and family life

and much, much more!

Log on today to check out Lifepath and our
special free classes.

www.lifepath.cc